LIVING LANGUAGE®

TERRA COGNITA™

IN THE KNOW IN

MEXICO and CENTRAL AMERICA

BUSINESS COMPANION. This unique business phrasebook provides a multitude of phrases and cultural information essential to working with foreign colleagues. The book includes phrases for general business situations common to all fields, industry-specific terms in over 25 fields, a two-way glossary, measurements, useful addresses, Web sites, and more. The audio CD includes over 500 phrases used in realistic, up-to-date business settings. Available in Chinese, German, and Spanish.

ULTIMATE COURSES. The comprehensive program covers conversation, grammar, reading, writing, and culture. Each of the 40 lessons begins with a dialogue and includes explanations of grammar and usage, vocabulary, and notes on customs and culture. Unique to this course are two sets of recordings: four hours in the target language for use with the manual, and four bilingual recordings ideal for learning on the go. Basic–Intermediate. French, German, Inglés, Italian, Japanese, Russian, Spanish, Portuguese, and Chinese.

ULTIMATE ADVANCED COURSES. Sequels to the Basic–Intermediate program, these courses include sections on business vocabulary and etiquette in addition to the dialogue-based lessons. Advanced. French, German, Inglés, Italian, Japanese, Russian, and Spanish.

COMPLETE BASIC COURSES (Level 1). The original, best-selling Living Language® program developed by U.S. government experts in 1946, revised and updated in 1993, includes three hours of recordings on cassette or compact disc, a manual, and a two-way, 20,000-word dictionary. Featuring a proven speed-learning method, the course progresses from words to phrases to complete sentences and dialogues. Recordings are done entirely in the target language. Beginner–Intermediate. French, German, Inglés, Italian, Japanese, Portuguese, Russian, and Spanish.

LIVING LANGUAGE® SKILL BUILDER: VERBS. This course teaches more than 150 conjugations through practical phrases and dialogues. The set includes four 60-minute bilingual cassettes and a 384-page text with 40 dialogues, exercises, and verb charts. Intermediate. French, German, Italian, and Spanish.

ADVANCED CONVERSATION COURSES. Four 60-minute cassettes in the target language feature more sophisticated dialogues, idiomatic expressions, and grammar. The accompanying 350-page conversation manual includes the transcript with English translations, verb charts, culture notes, and exercises to check one's progress. Advanced. French and Spanish.

BOOKS ALSO AVAILABLE SEPARATELY.

Living Language® publications are available at special discounts for bulk purchases for sales promotions or premiums, as well as for fund-raising or educational use. Special editions can be created in large quantities for special needs. For more information, write to: Special Sales Manager, Living Language, 280 Park Ave., New York, NY 10017.

At bookstores everywhere. You can also reach us on the Web at:
www.livinglanguage.com

300 West 49th Street Suite 314 New York, New York 10019 USA
Phone: 212.262.4529 Fax: 212.262.5789
E-mail: info@terracognita.com
www.terracognita.com   www.culturesavvy.com

Know Your World

Terra Cognita provides top quality cross-cultural training services and resources. The goal of our cross-cultural learning material is to help you build the awareness and skills to recognize and respect cultural differences you will encounter. Terra Cognita programs thereby ensure a successful adjustment to life in a new culture for expatriates and the skills necessary to succeed in international business.

Terra Cognita delivers cross-cultural learning with private seminars and workshops, with online learning modules, and with a variety of video, audio and printed material. Currently Terra Cognita programs meet the needs of expatriates and international business colleagues at various multinational companies, government agencies and educational institutions worldwide.

LIVE ABROAD! is an innovative video-based expatriate preparation program that covers the entire expatriate experience from preparing to go through the cultural adjustment process to the final return home.

WORK ABROAD! is a video-based program that explains and vividly recreates the cross-cultural dynamics of the international business environment.

CultureSavvy.com
Prepare to Live and Work Abroad

CULTURESAVVY is an online cross-cultural learning center that features streamed video. Over 50 learning modules guide the future expatriate and international business traveler in building cross-cultural skills. This site was developed by Arthur Andersen with Terra Cognita content. View the demo at www.culturesavvy.com.

For more information on Terra Cognita
and a wealth of articles and resources for cross-cultural learning,
visit our Web site at WWW.TERRACOGNITA.COM

VIDEOS   SEMINARS   ONLINE

LIVING LANGUAGE®
A Random House Company

IN THE KNOW IN

MEXICO and CENTRAL AMERICA

AN INDISPENSABLE CROSS-CULTURAL GUIDE TO WORKING AND LIVING ABROAD

WRITTEN BY

Jennifer Phillips

EDITED BY

Christopher Warnasch

Published by Living Language, A Random House Company,
New York, New York.

Living Language is a member of the Random House Information Group.
Random House, Inc. New York, Toronto, London, Sydney, Auckland

www.livinglanguage.com

Living Language and colophon are
registered trademarks of Random House, Inc.

Manufactured in the United States of America.

Design by Barbara M. Bachman
Illustrations by Adrian Hashimi

Library of Congress Cataloging-in-Publication Data available

ISBN 0-609-60817-7

10 9 8 7 6 5 4 3 2 1

First Paperback Edition

ACKNOWLEDGMENTS

Special thanks to Elicet Zafra, who provided assistance in the formidable task of gathering information on not just one country, but an entire region. Thanks as well to the people who generously shared their experiences and input, and to my editor, Chris Warnasch, for his expert guidance. No book is written in a vacuum, and this one would never have happened without the generous support of Richard Davis, with whom I continue a journey toward Terra Cognita. And finally, last on this list but not in my heart, to Jan, who provided the occasional much-needed kick in the seat and to my family for their support and encouragement.

And thanks to the rest of the Living Language team: Lisa Alpert, Elizabeth Bennett, Helen Tang, Elyse Tomasello, Zviezdana Verzich, Suzanne McGrew, Pat Ehresmann, Denise DeGennaro, Linda Schmidt, Marina Padakis, Barbara Bachman, and Fernando Galeano.

CONTENTS

CONTENTS

CONTENTS

Whether you're moving to Mexico or Central America or traveling there for business, it's essential that you know what to expect, and what will be expected of you. Cross-cultural awareness provides you with just that knowledge. Living Language® Terra Cognita™ *In the Know in Mexico and Central America* is designed to help both businesspeople and their families navigate the often complex waters of life in another culture. By culture we don't mean the Mayan ruins or the compiled works of Octavio Paz. Culture is the backdrop of every activity you engage in and every word you exchange. In Central America, you'll be dealing with a foreign culture every time you shake a colleague's hand, sit down to write an e-mail, get on a train, or even buy a loaf of bread. A list of "dos and don'ts" provides only part of the picture. A more thorough understanding of culture—what really motivates people's behaviors, attitudes, beliefs, and habits—will allow you, and any family members with you, to adapt with ease to both the social and business environments of Mexico and Central America.

This book was developed to be easy, practical, and comprehensive. You'll first get your bearings through some general background information about Mexico and Central America, such as its history, geography, political system, and social structure. This is no history text, though. The Background section is meant to be a brief survey that will familiarize you with some important landmarks you'll no doubt hear about or see. If something strikes you as interesting, the Background section will also serve you well as a way to get your feet wet in a particular area; we leave any further exploration of Central American history up to you.

Next you'll read an overview of Central American culture. For our purposes here, we've broken culture down into the following six categories: Time, Communication, Group Dynamics, Status and Hierarchy, Relationships, and Reasoning. Naturally, this provides only a general picture of the components of Central American culture, but a very practical picture, too. And even while using these generalizations, we can never forget that any culture is made of individuals, and individuals vary. Learning about these important general concepts, though, where differences and pitfalls abound, will better prepare you and your family for a more successful experience abroad.

The following section, Living Abroad, is meant to give you some insight about the issues that people face in other cultures. Here you'll learn what to expect as a businessperson, a family member, a parent, a child, an individual, or a teenager. This section applies to life in any other culture, and you'll find the insights invaluable. It will raise the kind of important questions you'll want to consider when preparing to make an adjustment to life abroad. Most importantly, it will prepare you to face some tough challenges, and then reap some wonderful benefits.

The following two sections of the book, Getting Around and Living & Staying in Mexico and Central America, are a comprehensive, step-by-step guide to everyday life in Central America. These are the issues that everyone must deal with, from driving and taking buses to shopping to social etiquette. These sections are full of easily organized information, practical lists, and essential tips. Everyone—single traveler, parent, or child—will benefit.

Next are two sections designed specifically for the businessperson. In Business Environment, you'll get an idea of the general principles that govern working in Mexico or Central America, from company values to chain of command, workspace, and women in business. Then, in Business Step-by-Step, you'll learn about the real essentials of doing business in Mexico or Central America, ranging from such important issues as speeches, presentations, and negotiations to such often overlooked but crucial details as business-card etiquette and making appointments.

Finally, we leave you with an introduction to the essentials of the Spanish language. While it is true that English is the lingua franca of global business, not everyone speaks it. More importantly, it cannot be denied that even a very basic knowledge of a foreign language can make a world of difference. This is no full-service language course; you won't be memorizing any irregular verbs or grammar rules. But you'll find that the minimal amount of time it takes to learn some basic social expressions and survival vocabulary will be recouped a hundred times over. Your Mexican or Central American colleagues and friends will be very appreciative that you've made an effort to learn just a little of their language. You'll find that the experience of another language is often its own reward, and you may even want to go further and learn to speak Spanish more fluently.

Please note that all data provided in this book is the most current available at the time of writing.

Good luck! (or *¡Buena suerte!*) and enjoy. We hope you find this course informative, practical, and enriching.

BACKGROUND

One of the first issues to deal with when speaking of Mexico or Central America is the question of what to call people from the various countries in that region. It can be problematic for people from the United States of America, as Mexicans and Central Americans are "Americans" too. To further complicate matters, claiming to be from the "United States" can be confused with being from the United States of Mexico. Even saying that you are from "North America" has its limitations, because Mexico, of course, is part of North America as well. U.S. citizens find themselves searching for a way to refer to themselves without needlessly offending someone.

In most cases it will be eminently obvious to our neighbors in the south that you are from the United States of America, not the United States of Mexico. The matter, then, boils down to how one presents oneself, not terminology. Unfortunately, Americans have a history of equating "American" with "superior," a sentiment that is understandably resented not only in Central America but around the world. Even those Americans who travel to Central America with the best of intentions and goodwill can find themselves battling the legacy of those who came before. It is necessary, therefore, to remember when you refer to yourself as "American" that you use that only as a designation of your citizenship and not as a weapon. Canadian readers, of course, have the luxury of citizenship in a country whose name cannot possibly be confused with that of any Central American country and no historical baggage to take with them to Central America.

In this book the word "American" will be used to identify citizens of the United States of America, and the words "America" and "U.S." will refer to that country. The term "Central American" will be used to identify generally those persons who live in the middle American countries.

Now let's move onto the term "Central America." Thus far in the book, and in the table of contents and chapter headings, you've seen "Mexico and Central America" spelled out separately, since "Central America" is generally not considered to include Mexico. However, for simplicity's sake more than any other reason, you'll find from this point forward that "Central America," for our purposes, includes Mexico as well as Guatemala, Honduras, Belize, El Salvador, Nicaragua, Costa Rica, and Panama. The term "Central America" was chosen rather than "Latin America," as the latter term has a much broader latitude and includes those people residing in South America as well. While the "Latin" culture is a common thread throughout both Central and South America, the focus of this book is solely Mexico and Central America. In addition, it should be noted that of all of the Central American countries, Belize alone uses English as its official language. Geographically speaking, of course, Belize falls within Central America; Spanish is the first language of many of its people and its roots are closely entwined with those of its neighbors.

Because Mexico is the largest Central American market and the destination of many American business travelers and expatriates, this book focuses primarily on that country, with supplemental information for other Central American countries. The information contained in this book is the most current available at the time of writing. Some Central American countries have gone through periods of political and economic instability, and foreign visitors have been affected, both inadvertently and by design. Readers are therefore urged to contact the Department of State and other sources of information for up-to-date information on issues of safety.

One final caveat is necessary. It goes without saying that each Central American country is a distinct entity with a proud national and cultural history. It would be unrealistic to expect that all people from any one country act and think the same, much less the peoples of different cultures. However, the countries of Central America do share a common cultural history and accordingly some generalizations can be made, especially when viewed as the counterfoil to American culture. As you travel through Central America it is important that you remember to respect the local culture and traditions of wherever you are.

MEXICO

Official Name:	**Estados Unidos Mexicanos (United Mexican States)**
Capital:	**México D.F. (Mexico City)**
Federal Flag:	**Green (religion), white (union), and red (independence) vertical bands with a centered emblem of an eagle on a cactus with a snake in its mouth**
National Anthem:	**"Himno Nacional de México" (National Anthem of Mexico)**
Area:	**756,006 sq mi (1,958,201 sq km)**
Highest Point:	**Pico de Orizaba (also known as Citlaltépetl), 18,410 ft (5,610 m)**

Lowest Point:	Near Mexicali, 33 ft (10 m) below sea level
Natural Resources:	Petroleum, silver, copper, gold, lead, zinc, natural gas, timber
Population (6/1998 est.):	98,552,776
Population Density (1996):	131 persons per sq mi
Population Growth (1998):	1.77%
Urban/Rural Distribution:	75% urban, 25% rural
Largest Cities:	Mexico City, Guadalajara, Netzahualcóyotl, Monterrey
Ethnicity:	60% mestizo (Spanish-Indian); 30% Indian (or predominantly Indian); 9% white; 1% other
Language:	Spanish; approximately 7% of the population uses Náhuatl, Maya, Zapotec, Mixtec, or another Indian language. There are over 50 languages and over 500 dialects in Mexico.
Literacy:	89.6% of population age 15 and over
Religions:	96% Roman Catholic, 3.6% Protestant, Jewish, Indian religions, other
Currency:	new peso = 100 centavos
GDP (1997 est.):	$694.3 billion
GDP per Capita (1997 est.):	$7,700
Inflation Rate (1997 est.):	15.7%

Major Trading Partners:	**United States, Canada, European Union, Japan**
Unemployment (3/1999):	**2.7%**
Employment by Industry:	**38.9% services; 21.8% retail/wholesale trade; 20.3% manufacturing; 6.2% government; 5.9% communications/transportation; 4.3% construction; 2.6% other**

THE LAND

There are any number of ways to divide Mexico geographically. The least complicated division gives Mexico six main regions: the Pacific northwest, the plateau of Mexico, the coastal plains of the Gulf of Mexico, the southern uplands, the Chiapas highlands, and the Yucatán Peninsula.

The Pacific Northwest

This generally dry region contains mountainous desert in the peninsula of Lower California, the region's westernmost area, yet it also contains some of Mexico's richest farmland. In the southern end of the Valley of California, near Mexicali, lies Mexico's lowest point at 33 ft (10 m) below sea level.

Plateau of Mexico

The plateau of Mexico is the largest of Mexico's regions and can be divided into five subregions.

The Cordillera Neovolcánica (Neo-Volcanic Chain), a string of active volcanoes, extends across the plateau's southern edge immediately south of Mexico City. The fertile volcanic soil receives enough rain to permit the cultivation of corn, beans, and other crops, making this an important agricultural region. Mexico's highest point, Pico de Orizaba (also known as Citlaltépetl), is found in this region, as is the largest lake, Lake Chapala, which covers 417 square miles.

The Mesa Central is the heart of Mexico and lies north of the Neo-Volcanic Chain. Mexico City, built on the site of the Aztec capital Tenochtitlán after the Spanish conquest, stands at the southern edge of the region. The Mesa Central is the country's leading center of culture, industry, and transportation. The western part of the Mesa Central, called the Bajio (flat), includes one of the most productive agricultural areas in the country as well as manufacturing centers such as Guadalajara, León, Querétaro, and San Luis Potosí.

The Meseta del Norte (northern plateau) extends from the Mesa Central north to the United States, making up more than half of the plateau of Mexico. The Mesa del Norte receives little rain except in the higher mountains. While frost is a severe threat to crops, irrigated areas such as Saltillo and Torreón support farming. There are rich deposits of metal ores in the low mountains of the Mesa del Norte. During the 1500s, the Spaniards established ranches to supply the miners with housing, beef, and mules. From these ranches in Durango and Chihuahua was born the tradition of the *vaqueros*, renowned for their skill in riding, roping cattle, and fighting Indians, skills taught to the American cowboy.

The Sierra Madre Occidental, a long mountain range that forms the western rim of the plateau of Mexico, is a natural barrier that made travel (and therefore commerce) difficult between the plateau and the western coast until the advent of the railroad and paved roads. This range has the most rugged landscape in Mexico, including Mexico's largest canyon, the Barranca del Cobre (The Canyon of Bronze), cut by the Urique River.

The Sierra Madre Oriental forms the plateau's eastern rims. With large deposits of coal and iron ore, this area is home to Mexico's steel industry in and around Monterrey.

The northern part of the Gulf coastal plain, north of Tampico, is dry, with tangled forests of low, thorny bushes and trees covering the plain. More rain falls to the south, allowing for farming, and a tropical rain forest in Tabasco. Mexico's longest River, the Río Bravo (which people to its north know as "the Rio Grande"), marks Mexico's border with the U.S. and is located in this region. There are also petroleum deposits beneath the plain and offshore and huge sulfur deposits near the Gulf of Mexico in the Isthmus of Tehuantepec.

The southern uplands are mainly steep ridges and deep gorges cut by mountain streams. There is also a large, hot, dry valley located south of the Neo-Volcanic Chain, drained by the Balsas River. The Sierra Madre del Sur rises southwest of the valley along the Pacific Ocean. Minimal farming takes place on the steep mountainsides.

The Chiapas highlands contain blocklike mountains that rise more than 9,000 ft (2,700 m) above sea level. Indians farm the plateaus of these mountains and modern farming techniques allow coffee, fruit, and other crops to be grown in the deep, broad river valleys.

The Yucatán Peninsula is a low limestone plateau with no rivers. The northwestern part of the region is dry bushland; the southern part is covered with tropical rain forests.

THE PEOPLE

The population of Mexico is 60% mestizo, a mixture of Spanish and Indian, 30% Indian, and 9% white. There are at least 54 different groups of native peoples, most of whom have their own language and cultural traditions. People in Mexico generally take pride in their native heritage, although native groups do sometimes face discrimination.

RELIGION

The vast majority of Mexicans are Roman Catholic. As you would expect, there are varying degrees of devotion, from the pious, for whom the Church provides the foundation of one's life, to the skeptical, for whom Catholic doctrines represent an old-fashioned way of life. However, no matter the level of devotion, Catholicism is deeply entwined with life in Mexico, and indeed throughout Central America. Even those who are non-practicing Catholics have their babies baptized and observe the principal Catholic rites, such as first communion, confirmation, and marriage.

The Catholic religion as it exists in Central America is really a fusion of Catholic doctrine and the religious beliefs of the indigenous people who were conquered by the Spanish. For the conquering Spanish, dominance was to be achieved not only militarily and politically, but also religiously. In fact, Hernán Cortés was accompanied by priests when he vanquished the capital city of Tenochtitlán. The conquerors destroyed temples and replaced them with churches and the conversion began.

At the time, most indigenous tribes worshiped many different gods who represented various aspects of nature; they were understandably reluctant to discard their gods in favor of the Catholic God. This religious gap was finally bridged by the appearance of the Virgin of Guadalupe. On December 12, 1531, an Aztec named Quauhtlatoatzin, baptized and renamed Juan Diego, was walking on Tepeyac Hill, a barren area north of Mexico City, looking for water for his sick uncle. Suddenly the Virgin Mary appeared to him and directed him to a spring. At the same place a few days later, the Virgin Mary again appeared to Juan Diego and told him that she desired a temple built there. When Juan Diego relayed the request to the Bishop, his story was not believed. Again the Virgin told Juan Diego to go see the Bishop and ask that a temple be built, and again he obeyed, to no avail. When the Virgin appeared yet again, Juan Diego asked her for a sign that he could give to the Bishop. The Virgin directed him to go gather some flowers, and Juan Diego found that red roses were suddenly blooming on the barren ground nearby. He wrapped the roses in his *tilma*, a rough blanket or cape, and took them to the Bishop. When he opened his *tilma*, the roses fell to the ground, revealing the image of the Virgin imprinted on the *tilma*. Upon examination, it was also discovered that the eyes of the Virgin contained a reflection of Juan Diego. Finally Juan Diego was believed, and a church was built, as she had requested.

The apparition of the Virgin Mary provided the connection between the gods of the indigenous peoples and the Catholic conquerors, since the Virgin had appeared to an Aztec and spoke to him in Náhuatl, his native language. Moreover, the site where she appeared was near a temple of the goddess Tonantzin, destroyed by the Spanish. Tonantzin was a manifestation of the Earth Mother, Coatlicue, which further served to meld native and Catholic beliefs.

The Virgin of Guadalupe remains a cornerstone of the special form of Catholicism that exists in Mexico today. Indeed, the Church declared Guadalupe the Patron of Mexico in 1737, she was named Queen of Mexico in 1895, and Pope Pius X crowned her Celestial Patron of Latin America in 1910. Pope John Paul II beatified Juan Diego in 1990.

Catholicism in Mexico and Central America is also unique in its veneration of saints to a greater degree than in most other Catholic areas. Like the Virgin, the saints helped to provide a link to native beliefs, since the Catholic Church was very adept at relating the Catholic saints to the native gods. The saints became the intermediaries who facilitated prayers to God, and each was assigned a specific area of concern. Thus the native custom of praying to a particular god for a specific reason was incorporated into Catholicism. Many cities have a patron saint, and the saints' feast days are cause for celebration.

MEXICO HISTORY IN BRIEF

C 2000 BC	**Village life developed in the Valley of Mexico.**
C AD 250–900	**Indian civilizations thrived during the Classic Period.**
C 900–1200	**The Toltec empire controlled the Valley of Mexico.**

c 1325-1350 The Aztec founded Tenochtitlán
(now Mexico City).

1519 Hernán Cortés founds La Villa Rica de la Vera
Cruz, the first Spanish settlement in Mexico in
April. In November, Cortés arrives in
Tenochtitlán and is received by Moctezuma II;
Cortés takes Moctezuma prisoner a few days
later.

1520 A religious festival at Tenochtitlán turns into the
Massacre of the Templo Mayor, also called the
Noche Triste (Night of Sorrow). Large numbers
of Spaniards trying to escape the city are killed.

1521 Hernán Cortés destroys Aztec defenses and
begins a 75-day siege on Tenochtitlán in May.
Tenochtitlán falls in August, completing Cortés's
conquest of the Aztec empire for Spain.

THE COLONIAL PERIOD

1530–1550	The first Viceroy of Mexico, Antonio de Mendoza.
1531	The apparition of the Virgin of Guadalupe.
1528	Carlos V of Spain establishes the Audiencia in Nueva España to handle local administration.
1522–1536	Explorers expand the empire in all directions.
1551	Founding of the Real y Pontífica Universidad de México, the first university in the Americas, in Mexico City.
1656	Inauguration of the first cathedral in Mexico.
1566	Martín Cortés leads a revolt of the conquistadors against the Spanish crown to protest the centralization of power, which threatened the local power of the conquistadors.
1810	The War for Independence begins, led by the priest Miguel Hidalgo y Costilla.
1811	Rebel leaders, including Hidalgo, are captured following their defeat in the battle of the Bridge of Calderón and sentenced to death. José María Morelos takes over the revolutionary effort.
1821	Mexico wins its independence from Spain.

POST-INDEPENDENCE

1822	The First Empire sees Augustín de Iturbide crowned Emperor Augustín I.
1823	Antonio López de Santa Anna begins a republican movement, forcing the abdication of Augustin I and instituting the Mexican Constitution. The Federal Republic of Mexico is born, with López as President.
1835	Texas declares itself a republic, independent of Mexico.

1846–48	López wages war on the United States, culminating in the Treaty of Guadalupe, giving Texas, New Mexico, and California to the U.S.
1855	A liberal government under Benito Juárez begins a period of reform.
1859	La Reforma, a series of reform mandates, lays the ground for the nationalization of Church property and freedom of worship and more, separating church and state, and checking the power of the Catholic Church.
1862	The Mexican National Army wins an unexpected victory against French invaders headed by Napoleon III in the battle of Puebla on May 5 (see Batalla de Puebla in the Holidays section).
1863	French troops occupy Mexico City.
1864	The Second Empire begins when Maximilian Habsburg of Austria becomes Emperor, aided by Napoleon III of France.
1867	As France's support wanes, Maximilian is captured and shot before a firing squad. Liberal forces led by Benito Juárez regain power and the Republic is reestablished.

PORFIRIO DÍAZ AND THE REVOLUTION

1876–80, 1884–1911	General Porfirio Díaz rules Mexico as dictator, maintaining a tight hold on power but bringing economic prosperity to Mexico.
1910–1911	Francisco I. Madero overthrows Díaz following an armed rebellion.
1911	The Zapatista movement begins during the Mexican Revolution, led by Emiliano Zapata, whose Plan de Ayala addresses agrarian

problems under the slogan *"tierra y libertad"* (land and liberty).

1913   During La Decena Trágica (the Tragic Ten) opposition forces lay siege to Mexico City; Madero is captured and assassinated.

1917   A revolutionary constitution is adopted and Venustiano Carranza is elected president.

1919   Emiliano Zapata is assassinated.

1920   The government begins making revolutionary social and economic reforms.

CONTEMPORARY MEXICO

1929   The National Revolutionary Party [now called the Institutional Revolutionary Party (PRI)], Mexico's first official political party, is formed.

1934   The government begins a major program of land distribution to farmers.

1938   Mexico takes over foreign oil company properties.

1953   Women receive the right to vote in all elections.

1968   Government troops put down student demonstrations in Mexico City.

1970s   Major new petroleum deposits are discovered along the coast of the Gulf of Mexico.

1985   Two earthquakes strike south-central Mexico, killing about 10,000 people.

1986   Mexico enters GATT (General Agreement on Tariffs and Trade).

1994   NAFTA (North American Free Trade Agreement) takes effect, providing for the gradual elimination of trade barriers between Mexico, the United States, and Canada.

| 1997 | The Institutional Revolutionary Party (PRI) loses its majority in the Chamber of Deputies for the first time. |
| 2000 | Vicente Fox of PAN (National Action Party) wins the presidential elections, unseating the PRI from the presidency for the first time since 1934. |

NOTED (AND NOTORIOUS) MEXICANS

MOCTEZUMA II (1480–1520)

The last Aztec emperor in Mexico, Moctezuma II welcomed Hernán Cortés when he arrived at Tenochtitlán, only to have his hospitality repaid with betrayal when Cortés took him prisoner.

SOR JUAN INÉS DE LA CRUZ (1651–1695)

Known as the first feminist in Mexican history, Sor Juan Inés de la Cruz was a genius who learned to read and write at the age of three; at age eight she wrote a short dramatic poem (*loa*) in honor of the blessed sacrament. Her best-known work was "First Dream," which was translated into English.

MIGUEL HIDALGO Y COSTILLA (1753–1811)

A Catholic priest in the village of Dolores, Hidalgo is known as the father of Mexican independence. In 1810, Hidalgo's call for the arrest of Dolores's *gachupines* (native Spaniards) sparked a revolution that freed Mexico from the yoke of Spain and ended the exploitation of the Mexicans by the Spanish. His cry of "*Mexicanos, Viva México*" became the anthem of Mexican independence.

GUADALUPE VICTORIA (1785–1843)

Mexico's first president, Victoria had been a military leader in Mexico's struggle for independence from Spain.

BENITO JUÁREZ (1806–1872)

Juárez became Mexico's first Indian president in 1858. A Zapotec who didn't speak Spanish as a child, Juárez first became a lawyer, then an official in the town of Oaxaca, and then the governor of Oaxaca. In 1862, Juárez successfully defended Mexico from invasion by French soldiers. His philosophy is found in his belief that "among nations and individuals, the respect for the rights of others is peace."

FRANCISCO I. MADERO (1873–1913)

Calling for the expulsion of President Porfirio Díaz as early as 1908, Madero was eventually installed as president of Mexico in 1911. He served until 1913, when he was overthrown by Victoriano Huerta and assassinated.

EMILIANO ZAPATA (1879–1919)

A rebel leader during the Mexican revolution, Zapata was assassinated in 1919 by Colonel Jesús Guajardo under the orders of the Mexican president Carranza.

PANCHO VILLA (1878–1923)

Born Doroteo Arango in Durango, Pancho Villa was a Mexican rebel general during the Mexican Revolution. He sought unsuccessfully to control Mexico after the fall of President Porfirio Díaz in 1911. He led the only foreign invasion onto mainland U.S. soil at Columbus, New Mexico, in 1916.

DIEGO RIVERA (1886–1957)

A modernist artist, Rivera had a political edge to his work. He was born in the city of Guanajuato and spent most of the revolutionary years studying and working in Europe. In 1921, Rivera returned to Mexico and became the most popular of the "big three" muralists in Mexico.

OCTAVIO PAZ (1914–1998)

Octavio Paz was awarded the Nobel Prize for Literature in 1990. He was a political activist as well as a writer. Paz angrily resigned his position as ambassador to India following the 1968 student massacre at Tlatelco.

POLITICS AND GOVERNMENT

Mexico's political system is shaped by the Federal Constitution of the United Mexican States, proclaimed on February 5, 1917. Mexico has 31 states and one federal district that are responsible for internal regulation, but are united in a federal republic. The federal government consists of the executive, legislative, and judicial branches.

Administrative Divisions

AGUASCALIENTES	MORELOS
BAJA CALIFORNIA	NAYARIT
BAJA CALIFORNIA SUR	NUEVO LEÓN
CAMPECHE	OAXACA
CHIAPAS	PUEBLA
CHIHUAHUA	QUERÉTARO
COAHUILA	QUINTANA ROO
COLIMA	SAN LUIS POTOSÍ
DISTRITO FEDERAL	SINALOA
DURANGO	SONORA
ESTADO DE MÉXICO	TABASCO
GUANAJUATO	TAMAULIPAS
GUERRERO	TLAXCALA
HIDALGO	VERACRUZ
JALISCO	YUCATÁN
MICHOACÁN	ZACATECAS

Executive Branch

Mexico's head of state and government is the President, who is elected by popular vote to a six-year term. The Cabinet is appointed by the president with the consent of the Senate.

Legislative Branch

The *Congreso de la Unión* (National Congress) has two chambers: the *Cámara de Diputados* (Chamber of Deputies) and the *Cámara de Senadores* (Senate). The Chamber of Deputies is composed of 500 representatives elected to three-year terms. Three hundred of the deputies are elected by plurality and two hundred are elected by a system of proportional representation.

The Senate is composed of four senators from each state and the federal district elected to six-year terms. Three of the four senators are elected by simple majority and the remaining seat is given to the second majority.

Judicial Branch

The judicial branch is made up of the *Corte Suprema de Justicia* (Supreme Court of Justice) and circuit and district courts. Supreme Court justices are appointed by the Senate following presidential nomination.

Political Parties

PARTIDO REVOLUCIONARIO INSTITUCIONAL—PRI (Insttutional Revolutionary Party). A powerful political machine, the PRI has dominated Mexican politics since 1929. Until Vincente Fox's election in 2000, every president since 1934 had been from the PRI. The PRI has wide support in all important areas, including labor unions, farmers, industry, business, and the media.

PARTIDO DE LA REVOLUCIÓN DEMOCRÁTICA—PRD (Democratic Revolutionary Party). The strongest party to the left of the PRI, the PRD has gained support from the working class and farmers.

PARTIDO ACCIÓN NACIONAL—PAN (National Action Party). The PAN, politically more conservative than the PRI, has supporters in conservative Catholics, traditional landed families, and business. This is the party of Vincente Fox, the first president outside the PRI since 1934.

HOLIDAYS AND CELEBRATIONS

January 1	Año Nuevo	New Year's Day
January 6	Día de los Santos Reyes	Day of the Three Kings (Epiphany)
February 5	Día de la Constitución	Constitution Day
March 21	Aniversario de Benito Juárez	Benito Juárez's Birthday
March/April	Semana Santa	Holy Week (Maundy Thursday, Good Friday, Holy Saturday, Easter)
May 1	Día del Trabajo	Day of Work (Labor Day)
May 5	Día de la Batalla de Puebla	Day of the Battle of Puebla (Cinco de Mayo)
September 1	President's state of the nation address (sometimes on November 1)	
September 16	Día de la Independencia	Independence Day
October 12	Día de la Raza	Day of the Race (Columbus Day)
November 1	Todos los Santos	All Saints' Day
November 2	Día de los Muertos	Day of the Dead (All Souls' Day)
November 20	Día de la Revolución	Day of the Revolution
December 8	La Immaculada Concepción	Immaculate Conception
December 12	Fiesta de Nuestra Señora de Guadalupe	Festival of Our Lady of Guadalupe
December 25	Navidad	Christmas

In addition to these major holidays, there are many other religious and traditional celebrations that are important in different cities and regions. Cities and villages celebrate the feast day of their patron saint, and non-public holidays for almost everyone (mothers, fathers, children, teachers, etc.). In a country where mothers are revered, the absenteeism rate on Mother's Day (May 10) is so high that many businesses simply close down for the day.

There are as many traditions as there are holidays, far too many to cover thoroughly. Christmas and the *Quinceaños* (fifteenth birthday) are two occasions that warrant a more detailed description.

The Christmas Season

Christmas festivities begin with *Las Posadas*, which are nine consecutive days of candlelight processions starting on December 16, in remembrance of Mary and Joseph's search for lodging before the birth of Jesus. Groups of people representing the Virgin Mary, Joseph, angels, the three kings, shepherds, and shepherdesses participate in the parade of *Santos Peregrinos* (Holy Pilgrims) to designated homes, singing a traditional litany requesting shelter for the night. They are rejected at the first and second homes they come to, but at the third house they are told that while there is no room in the *posada* (inn), they are welcome to stay in the stable. The home in which the *Santos Peregrinos* finally find sanctuary is decorated with *nacimientos* (nativity scenes), but the merriment of the *posadas* includes breaking the *piñata* full of candy, fruit, cookies, chocolates, peanuts, and sugar canes, not to mention the food!

Las Pastorelas are the shepherds' plays that are performed throughout the entire holiday season, held in both public squares and theaters. *Pastorelas* are light-humored dramatizations of the shepherds' journey to Bethlehem to visit the newborn Christ. The audience sees the creation, the fall of Lucifer, the fall of Adam and Eve, and the formation of the seven deadly sins. Then comes the angel who announces the birth of Christ to the shepherds. As the shepherds travel to Bethlehem they are plagued by the devil's mischief. These encounters are chronicled, ending with the shepherds' safe arrival at the side of the manger to worship Jesus.

El nacimiento is the nativity scene and is the centerpiece in most

Mexican homes during the holidays, complete with the three Magi, the shepherds, the Virgin Mary, Joseph, the star, all the animals, and the baby Jesus. To represent evil forces the serpent and a grotesque Lucifer may be found in the shadows. The nativity scenes may occupy an entire room or may simply be a small scene under a Christmas tree.

Noche Buena (Christmas Eve) is the day when the baby Jesus is placed into *el nacimiento* (the manger), a great honor. A *misa de gallo* (Rooster's Mass) is celebrated, after which families return home for a traditional Christmas dinner. This dinner may include the traditional *mole, pozole, tostadas, atole, ponche* (hot fruit punch), *sidra* (sparkling cider), and *refrescos* (soft drinks), or it may be a more exotic feast including *bacalao a la vizcaina* (Biscayan cod) and *revoltijo de romeritos* (wild greens in mole sauce). Some people have a *baile* (dance party) with *piñatas* and *luces de Belen* (sparklers), and sometimes gift giving. The *baile* is liable to continue into the next day. Christmas day is usually a day to rest and relax from the previous festivities and enjoy eating *el recalentado* (leftovers). Children make their holiday wish lists, addressed to the baby Jesus, who delivers them by way of the Three Wise Men on January 6. There is also a widely popular belief in Santa Claus among Mexican children, especially in urban areas.

Los Santos Inocentes (the Day of the Holy Innocents) takes place on December 28 to commemorate the slaughter of all male infants by King Herod in order to kill the baby Jesus. In Mexico, however, the day is celebrated similar to the American April Fool's Day, with jokes and pranks. The usual trick is to ask a friend for cash or something of value; he who falls for the trick is rewarded with teasing and, if he's lucky, a piece of candy.

Los Reyes Magos (Three Kings Day, or Epiphany) is celebrated on January 6, the day when the Wise Men arrived in Bethlehem with gifts for the Baby Jesus. This is the day when all children in Mexico anxiously await the gifts that they had requested from the baby Jesus on Christmas. In some parts of Mexico it is customary to leave out shoes so the Three Kings may put the gifts inside. On this day most people have a *Rosca de Reyes*, a crown-shaped sweet bread decorated with candied fruits and with a tiny figure of a baby hidden inside. Everyone who visits has to cut a slice of the *Rosca de Reyes*; the person who gets the slice with the baby is obligated to host another party on or before Candlemas (February 2), the official end to the holiday season.

Quinceaños *(Fifteenth Birthday)*

The *Quinceaños* celebration is a young lady's fifteenth birthday. This celebration is almost as important as a wedding celebration because it symbolizes the transition from a girl to a woman, some say of marriageable age.

Although the origins of the *Quinceaños* remain somewhat mysterious, it dates from pre-colonial times. Some say the tradition came from an Aztec rite of passage into womanhood. An alternate possibility is that the *Quinceaños* derives from the Toltec and Maya Indian ceremony honoring girls as future mothers. Whatever its origins, its current significance derives from the Catholic Church.

Traditionally, the *Quinceaños* is celebrated with a *Misa de acción de gracias* (Thanksgiving Mass), at which the honoree (called the *quinceañera*) wears a pastel gown. She may be accompanied by close friends acting as *damas* (maids) and *chambelanes* (chamberlains) and is escorted to the altar by her partner or parents.

Depending on the economic means of the *quinceañera*'s parents and godparents, the birthday girl has the option to go on a *viaje* (trip) or have a *fiesta*. While many *quinceañeras* choose the *viaje*, the traditional choice is a *fiesta* which allows friends and relatives to gather to celebrate this special event, and a banquet hall is rented, or a patio, corral, or outside area is cleared in preparation. The girl's *padrinos* (godparents) often sponsor the festivities, providing food, music, or even the dress for the occasion. The *quinceañera* makes her grand entrance with her attendants, then she dances a waltz with her father, then with her partner. This is followed by a formal toast and the cutting of the cake, and finally music, eating, and general revelry.

The American sweet sixteen party pales in comparison to the *Quinceaños*. This is truly a major event in a girl's life, and, like weddings and funerals, the fact that it occurs on a weekday is no excuse not to attend if you're invited.

EDUCATION

Educational System

The educational system in Mexico today is the result of the sweeping reforms of the National Agreement on Education in 1992. The Agreement sought to bring together the federal and local governments in a concerted effort to broaden and improve educational services throughout the country, focusing especially on the regions and social groups with poor educational systems. In the years since the Agreement, significant progress has been made, and Mexico has seen an increase from 72% to 85% in primary school completion and enrollment in secondary school has doubled.

The educational system in Mexico consists of three levels: primary school, *secundaria* (junior high), *preparatoria* (senior high) and *universidad* (university). Primary (six years) and secondary (three years) school attendance is mandatory.

Educational Philosophy

Whereas American schools teach concepts and their application, emphasizing problems solving skills, Mexican schools lean more toward deductive reasoning. Grades are based mainly on examinations rather than class participation or homework, so students learn to focus on recalling information rather than the practical application of knowledge.

In the classroom itself you will find differences between the United States and Mexico. Mexican students have a more regimented classroom environment and learn to conform more than Americans, who are allowed more latitude for self-expression and challenging of ideas.

Mexican students generally receive a broader education when Americans begin to specialize. The result is a Mexican graduate with an excellent general knowledge about the world and current events but limited practical knowledge, and an American graduate with practical knowledge of a specific area and problem-solving skills, but limited general knowledge of other topics.

BELIZE

BACKGROUND

Official Name:	Belize (formerly British Honduras)
Capital:	Belmopan (The capital was moved inland from Belize City because of hurricane damage in 1961.)
Federal Flag:	Royal blue with a narrow red horizontal stripe top and bottom and a centered white circle bearing the coat of arms surrounded by a green garland
Area:	8.867 sq mi (22,960 sq km)
Highest Point:	Victoria Peak, 3,805 ft (1,160 m)
Lowest Point:	Caribbean Sea (sea level)
Natural Resources:	Arable land, timber, fish
Population (7/1998 est.):	230,160
Population Growth (1998 est.):	2.42%
Largest Cities:	Belize City, Orange Walk Town, San Ignacio/Santa Elena
Ethnicity:	44% mestizo, 30% Creole, 11% Maya, 7% Garifuna, 8% other
Language:	English (official), Spanish, Mayan, Garifuna (Carib)
Literacy:	70.3%
Religions:	62% Roman Catholic; 30% Protestant (Anglican, Methodist, Mennonite, Seventh-Day Adventist,

Pentecostal, Jehovah's Witnesses, other); 2% none; 6% other

Currency: Belize dollar (Bz$) = 100 cents

Economic Overview: Traditionally based on forestry (dogwood, mahogany and chicle), Belize's economy is now based on agriculture, with tourism, construction, dairy and livestock gaining greater importance. Belize faces a growing trade deficit and high unemployment.

GDP (1997 est.): $680 million

GDP per Capita (1997 est.): $3,000

Inflation Rate (1997 est.): 1%

Major Trading Partners: United States, European Union (mainly the United Kingdom), Mexico

Unemployment (1997): 13%

Employment by Industry: 30% agriculture; 16% services; 15.4% government; 11.2% commerce; 10.3% manufacturing

THE LAND AND CLIMATE

Belize has a flat coastal plain, much of it covered with mangrove swamp. A large part of the mainland is forested, and there are low mountains in the south. Its climate is subtropical, very hot and humid, but tempered by trade winds, with a long rainy season lasting from May to February.

THE PEOPLE

Belize is home to a wide variety of ethnic and religious groups, cultures, and languages. Sharing the ethnic majority are the mestizos and Creoles. Ethnic minority groups include Maya, Garifuna, Lebanese, Chinese, and Eastern Indian. Intermarriage among different racial groups has blurred racial lines.

Mestizos are the descendants of Spaniards (and other Europeans) who intermarried with the Indians. Creoles are the descendants of African slaves. Garifuna immigrated to Belize from the Honduran Bay Islands and trace their roots back to a combination of African slaves, Carib Indians, and Europeans. There are three groups of Maya in Belize—Yucatec, Mopan, and Ketchi—who originate from different parts of Central America. The Maya are considered to be the poorest group in the country.

Mennonites

There are six Mennonite communities in the Orange Walk and Cayo districts. The Mennonites immigrated to Belize from Manitoba, Canada and Mexico beginning in the late 1950s. They retain their traditional religious beliefs, and maintain their own schools, churches, and financial institutions.

BELIZE HISTORY IN BRIEF

1000 BC—AD 900	Maya civilizations flourish then eventually disappear.
1502	Christopher Columbus sails along the coast of Central America.
1638	British woodcutters settled in Costa Rica, begin illegally harvesting the timber in Spanish domains. "Baymen"—mostly British sailors, buccaneers, and pirates—begin settling in Belize and

	torment Spanish galleons bound for Central America with cargoes of gold and silver.
1763, 1786	Failing to expel either the loggers or the baymen, Spain signs two treaties allowing them to remain in exchange for protection from pirates.
1786	Britain appoints a Superintendent for the territory.
1840	Belize is declared a colony of British Honduras.
1862	The territory is formally named a British colony, administered by the governor of Jamaica.
1964	The colonial status (Crown Colony) is discontinued and Belize becomes self-governed.
1973	The country's name is changed from British Honduras to Belize.
1981	On September 21, Belize declares its independence from Britain. However, Guatemala continues to claim Belize as part of its territory.
1984	The United Democratic Party (UDP), led by Manuel Esquivel, running on a free trade platform, defeats the People's United Party (PUP) in national elections.
1989	The People's United Party is returned to power by a narrow margin.
1991	Guatemala recognizes Belize's sovereignty and abandons its territorial claim, although some tension remains.
1993	The British announce that they will withdraw their forces from Belize within 15

months. The June election returns the UDP to power; the UDP is forced to raise taxes to cover fiscal mismanagement by the PUP.

1994	British troops depart from Belize on January 1.
1997	Belizean–United States anti-drug forces stage two raids off the coast.

POLITICS AND GOVERNMENT

There are six administrative districts in Belize: Belize, Cayo, Corozal, Orange Walk, Stann Creek, and Toledo. The country is a parliamentary democracy with Her Majesty Queen Elizabeth II as the constitutional head of state. Her representative in Belize is the Governor-General, who is appointed by the Queen and who must be a Belizean.

The Prime Minister and Cabinet make up the executive branch of government. The Prime Minister is appointed by the Governor-General; the Cabinet is appointed by the Governor-General on the advice of the Prime Minister.

The legislative branch is a bicameral National Assembly consisting of a Senate and House of Representatives. The Senate has eight members who are appointed to five-year terms. The 29 members of the House of Representatives are elected by direct popular vote to five-year terms. General elections are held at least every five years; the Prime Minister has the right to request that the Governor-General dissolve the House of Representatives, which can result in elections in less than five years.

The judicial branch consists of a supreme court and magistrate courts in each district. Each district also has a locally elected seven-member town board (except Belize City, which has a nine-member city council).

Political Parties

PEOPLE'S UNITED PARTY—PUP
UNITED DEMOCRATIC PARTY—UDP

NATIONAL HOLIDAYS

January 1	New Year's Day
March 9	Baron Bliss Day
March/April	Holy Week (Good Friday, Holy Saturday, Easter, Easter Monday)
May 1	Labor Day
May 24	Commonwealth Day
September 10	St. George's Caye Day
September 21	Independence Day
October 12	Columbus Day
November 19	Garifuna Settlement Day
December 25	Christmas Day
December 26	Boxing Day

COSTA RICA

BACKGROUND

Official Name:	Republic of Costa Rica
Capital:	San José
Federal Flag:	Five horizontal bands of blue, white, red (double width), white, and blue, with the coat of arms in a white disk on the left side of the flag

Area	19,730 sq mi (51,100 sq km)
Highest Point:	Cerro Chirripo, 12,496 ft (3,810 m)
Lowest Point:	Pacific Ocean (sea level)
Natural Resources:	Hydropower potential
Population (7/1998 est.):	3,604,642
Population Growth (1998 est.):	1.95%
Largest Cities:	San José, Alajuela, Puntarenas, Limón, Cartago
Ethnicity:	96% white (including mestizo); 2% black; 1% Indian; 1% Chinese
Language:	Spanish (English-speaking minority)
Literacy:	94.8%
Religions:	95% Roman Catholic
Currency:	1 Costa Rican colón = 100 céntimos
Economic Overview:	Costa Rica has a stable economy that depends largely on tourism and the export of bananas, coffee, and other agricultural products. Costa Rica faces inflation and deficit challenges, but recent foreign investment will help stimulate employment and growth.
GDP (1997 est.):	$19.6 billion
GDP per Capita (1997 est.):	$5,500
Inflation Rate (1997 est.):	11.2%
Major Trading Partners:	United States, Japan, European Union, Central America, Venezuela

Unemployment (1997):	5.7%, plus heavy under-employment
Employment by Industry:	35% industry and commerce; 33% government; 27% agriculture; 4% other

THE LAND AND CLIMATE

Costa Rica's topography consists of a rugged mountainous central region flanked by eastern and western coastal plains. The climate varies from mild in the central mountains to tropical and subtropical in the coastal areas. Costa Rica's rainy season lasts from May to November. The country suffers a host of natural hazards, including active volcanoes, occasional earthquakes, hurricanes along the Atlantic coast, and frequent flooding in the lowlands.

THE PEOPLE

Unlike most of its Central American neighbors, Costa Rica's population is mainly of European, primarily Spanish, rather than mestizo descent. The indigenous Indian populations were decimated by the Spaniards, and today's indigenous population is only 1%. While most of the population speaks Spanish, a small number of people descended from Jamaican workers who immigrated to Costa Rica in the nineteenth century speak English as their native language.

COSTA RICAN HISTORY IN BRIEF

1500	Spaniards first come to Costa Rica.
1502	Christopher Columbus lands near Limón on the Atlantic Coast.

1522	The Spaniards discover the Nicoya Peninsula in Costa Rica and settle in the Central Valley.
1539	Costa Rica becomes known as the "rich coast" (costa rica) because the Spaniards are given so much gold by the natives.
1563	Cartago is founded.
1717	Settlers from Cartago found Heredian.
1737	San José is founded.
1750	The population reaches approximately 2,500 and is divided into 500 family groups.
1821	Costa Rica and other Central American provinces declare their independence from Spain and form the Central American Federation. The first constitution, the Pacto de Concordia, is adopted, and the first elections are held in December.
1824	The first chief of state of Free Costa Rica, Juan Mora Fernández, is elected by Congress. He builds roads and schools, gives land grants to anyone who would plant coffee, and promotes industry and commerce.
1838	Under the administration of chief of state Braulio Carrillo, Costa Rica withdraws from the Central American Federation and proclaims itself a sovereign state.
1848	A declaration of absolute independence as a sovereign state is again issued by Costa Rica.
1850	Costa Rica is recognized as an independent state by Spain.
1856	William Walker, an American adventurer, invades Costa Rica.
1870–82	Tomás Guardia heads a military dictatorship in Costa Rica.
1899	The first totally free elections are held, marking

the beginning of an era of progress toward a truly popular government.

1913　　　The system of direct vote is established.

1925　　　Secret balloting in elections begins.

1945–74　The presidency alternates between conservative and liberals, while the Liberal National Party (PLN) dominates the Legislature.

1948　　　A 44-day civil war breaks out following an uprising led by José Figueres in the wake of a disputed presidential election.

1949　　　A new constitution is initiated by the victorious junta; it includes the guarantee of free elections with universal suffrage and the abolition of the army.

1953　　　Figueres, now a national hero, is elected president.

1978　　　Rodrigo Carazo Odio, leader of a four-party coalition called the Unity Party, wins the presidency in February; his tenure is marked by a disastrous decline in the economy.

1984　　　Democratic Costa Rica is besieged by several problems such as the armed conflict in neighboring Nicaragua and of El Salvador's threats to interfere with the national political process when the nation faces a dangerously low-level economic condition.

1985　　　The first U.S. military advisers train the Costa Rican National Guard.

1986　　　Oscar Arias Sánchez wins the national elections on a neutralist platform. He initiates a policy of preventing the Nicaraguan Contra rebels from using Costa Rican territory to train and hide from Nicaraguan government forces.

1987	Arias travels to Washington, D.C., and urges the president to discontinue aid to the Contras of Nicaragua. Arias receives the Nobel Prize for Peace as an architect of the Peace Plan for Central America .
1990	Rafael Calderón wins the presidential election.
1994	The presidential election is won by José María Figueres Olsen of the National party in February, proposing more government intervention in the economy.
1998	Miguel Rodríguez of the Social Christian Unity Party becomes president.

POLITICS AND GOVERNMENT

Costa Rica is a democratic republic with executive, legislative, and judicial branches of government. The executive branch consists of the president and two vice presidents, who are elected by popular vote, and a 19-member Cabinet selected by the president.

Members of the 57-seat unicameral *Asamblea Legislativa* (Legislative Assembly) are elected to four-year terms by popular vote. Judicial power is exercised by the *Corte Suprema* (Supreme Court), whose 22 justices are elected by the *Asamblea Legislativa* to renewable eight-year terms.

Costa Rica has seven *provincias* (provinces): Alajuela, Cartago, Guanacaste, Heredia, Limón, Puntarenes, and San José. *Provincias* are headed by governors, who are appointed by the president, but there is little provincial power.

By mandate of the country's 1949 constitution, Costa Rica has no standing military and maintains only domestic police and security forces.

Political Parties

Costa Rica has more than 20 political parties. Some of the largest are:

Fuerza Democrática—FD (Democratic Force)
Partido de Liberación Nacional—PLN
   (National Liberation Party)
Movimento Nacional—ML
   (National Movement)
Partido Unidad Social Cristiana—PUSC
   (Social Christian Unity Party)

NATIONAL HOLIDAYS

January 1	Año Nuevo	New Year's Day
March/April	Semana Santa	Holy Week (Maundy Thursday, Good Friday, Holy Saturday, Easter)
April 11	National Hero's Day	
May 1	Día del Trabajo	Day of Work (Labor Day)
July 25	Guanacaste Province's Annexation Day	
August 2	Virgin of Los Angeles Day	
August 15	Día de la Madre	Mother's Day
September 15	Día de la Independencia	Independence Day
October 12	Día de la Raza	Day of the Race (Columbus Day)
December 25	Navidad	Christmas

EL SALVADOR

BACKGROUND

Official Name:	Republic of El Salvador
Capital:	San Salvador
Federal Flag:	Three horizontal bands of blue, white and blue with the national coat of arms centered in the white band
Area:	8,124 sq mi (21,041 sq km)
Highest Point:	Cerro El Pital, 8,954 ft (2,730 m)
Lowest Point:	Pacific Ocean (sea level)
Natural Resources:	Hydro and geothermal power, petroleum
Population (7/1998 est.):	5,752,067
Population Growth (1998 est.):	1.57%
Largest Cities:	San Salvador, San Miguel, Ahuachapán
Ethnicity:	94% mestizo; 5% Indian; 1% white
Language:	Spanish, Nahua (Indian language)
Literacy:	71.5%
Religions:	75% Roman Catholic; Protestantism growing
Currency:	1 Salvadoran colon = 100 centavos
Economic Overview:	El Salvador's economy has rebounded from the economic devastation that was the result of the civil war from 1979 to 1990. Conservative fiscal policies implemented in 1997, including a fixed exchange rate, improved foreign investment. Inflation fell to 2% and exports

reached record levels. Continued
privatization is expected to
strengthen the economy.

GDP (1997 est.):	$17.8 billion
GDP per Capita (1997 est.):	$3,000
Inflation Rate (1997 est.):	2%
Major Trading Partners:	United States, Central America, Venezuela, Japan
Unemployment (1997):	7.7%
Employment by Industry:	40% agriculture; 16% commerce; 15% manufacturing; 13% government; 9% financial services; 6% transportation; 1% other

THE LAND AND CLIMATE

El Salvador can be separated into three regions. In the south is the coastal belt with narrow, fertile plains along the Pacific coast. The Central Region, where three-fourths of Salvadorans live, has agricultural land as well as hosting most of El Salvador's industry, and contains valleys and plateaus. The northern interior highlands' main feature is the Sierra Madre mountain range, composed of hardened lava and volcanic ash.

El Salvador's climate is tropical, with a rainy season lasting from May to October. El Salvador is known as the Land of Volcanoes, and experiences frequent and at times disastrous earthquakes and volcanic activity.

THE PEOPLE

El Salvador is one of Central America's poorest, smallest, and most densely populated countries. When the Spanish settled in El Salvador, they subdued the Pipil, the dominant indigenous tribe. Under the Spanish influence, most of the indigenous people left their own customs and culture to adapt to those of the Spanish conquerors. The people of El Salvador today are almost entirely mestizo, of Spanish and Indian descent.

EL SALVADOR HISTORY IN BRIEF

By 3000 BC	Chorotega tribes have migrated to El Salvador from central Mexico.
AD 100–1000	Western El Salvador is part of the Maya empire, occupied by a Maya tribe called the Pokoman, who build limestone pyramids in the hills.
1000s	The warlike Pipil, related to the Aztecs of Mexico, arrive in El Salvador and take over the western part of the country from the Pokoman. By the 1500s, the Pipil have conquered almost all of present-day El Salvador.
1524	Spanish conquistadors, under the leadership of Pedro de Alvarado, arrive in El Salvador and subdue the Pipil.
1525	Alvarado founds the city of San Salvador. Three years later, it is moved to its present site because of earthquakes.
1552	The Spanish establish the city and province of Sonsonate; San Salvador and Sonsonate are governed by the captain general of Guatemala.
1786	San Salvador becomes a governorship. Spanish colonists in Central America begin to become impatient with Spain's administration of the colonies.

1811	José Matías Delgado and Manuel José Arce lead an unsuccessful revolt against Spanish rule in San Salvador. A similar rebellion fails in 1814.
1821	The captain general of Guatemala declares Central America independent from Spain. He tries to unite Central America with the newly formed Mexican empire. San Salvador decides not to join the Mexicans.
1823	The Mexican empire collapses. Leaders of the region form the United Provinces of Central America, including San Salvador and Sonsonate, Honduras, Guatemala, Nicaragua, and Costa Rica. Arce is voted president of the new federation.
late 1820s	Liberal and conservative forces battle for control of the federation.
1829	Liberals in San Salvador rebel against Arce's rule.
1830	Under Francisco Morazán, a liberal army defeats the federation. Arce resigns and Morazán becomes president.
late 1830s	Peasant uprisings and conflicts between liberals and conservatives tear the federation apart. By 1839, only San Salvador remains a member.
1840	Salvadoran leaders found the Republic of El Salvador, including San Salvador and Sonsonate.
1840–85	Liberal and conservative forces again compete for power, sometimes engaging in war. Heads of state and government policies change frequently and unpredictably.
after 1885	The coffee industry flourishes. The government stabilizes but continues to be controlled by a few wealthy families.
1931	El Salvador's first elected president, Arturo Araujo, is thrown out of office when General

	Maximiliano Hernández Martínez seizes control of the government.
1931–44	Martínez rules as both military dictator and president, ruthlessly suppressing all political opposition.
1944–1970s	A series of military takeovers and short-lived governments destroys the country's political stability. During the 1970s, the government adopts harsh measures to silence its critics.
1969	El Salvador attacks Honduras in the short but bitter Soccer War. The Organization of American States negotiates a settlement of the border dispute.
late 1970s	Opposition to the government takes the form of guerrilla and terrorist action.
1978	The army kills 30 antigovernment protesters.
1979	A council of military officers takes control of the government and promises reform. José Napoleón Duarte is a civilian member of the council.
1980	The new government continues the repressive policies of the former regime, and violence between government and guerrilla forces becomes an open civil war. Duarte is appointed president.
1982	Duarte's party loses seats in the Constituent Assembly and he resigns from the presidency.
1984	Duarte is elected president.
1988	Fighting continues in El Salvador. Government forces are backed by the United States, and the antigovernment forces receive some aid from communists in Cuba and Nicaragua. Both sides are accused of assassinations, torture, and other violations of human rights.
1989	Alfredo Cristiani of the right wing ARENA Party

is elected president and calls for talks between the government and the guerrillas, which continue for two months until FMLN (Farabundo Martí National Liberation Front) forces stage an offensive across El Salvador.

1990 The United Nations becomes involved in mediating peace between the Salvadorian government and the guerrillas.

1992 The government and the FMLN sign a peace agreement; the war officially ends with the disbanding of FMLN forces and a reduction in El Salvador's armed forces.

1993 New national and local elections are held; Armando Calderón Sol of ARENA is elected President.

POLITICS AND GOVERNMENT

The Republic of El Salvador consists of 14 *departamentos* (departments):

AHUACHAPÁN	MORAZÁN
CABAÑAS	SAN MIGUEL
CHALATENANGO	SAN SALVADOR
CUZCATLÁN	SANTA ANA
LA LIBERTAD	SAN VICENTE
LA PAZ	SONSONATE
LA UNIÓN	USULUTÁN

The government includes executive, legislative, and judicial branches. The executive branch consists of the president and vice president, who are elected on the same ticket by popular vote for five-year terms, and the Council of Ministers.

The legislative branch is the unicameral *Asamblea Legislativa*

(Legislative Assembly), whose 84 members are elected by direct popular vote to three-year terms. The *Corte Suprema* (Supreme Court) forms the judicial branch; its judges are selected by the *Asamblea Legislativa*.

Political Parties

PARTIDO ALIANZA REPUBLICANA NACIONALISTA—
ARENA (Nationalist Republican Alliance)

PARTIDO CONVERGENCIA DEMOCRÁTICA—PCD
(Democratic Convergence)

PARTIDO DE CONCILIACIÓN NACIONAL—PCN
(National Conciliation Party)

PARTIDO DEMÓCRATA CRISTIANO—PDC
(Christian Democratic Party)

PARTIDO DEMÓCRATA—PD (Democratic Party)

PARTIDO FRENTE FARABUNDO MARTÍ PARA LA
LIBERACIÓN NACIONAL—FMLN
(Farabundo Martí National Liberation Front)

PARTIDO LIBERAL DEMOCRÁTICO—PLD
(Democratic Liberal Party)

PARTIDO POPULAR LABORISTA—PPL (Labor Party)

PARTIDO UNIÓN SOCIAL CRISTIANO—USC
(Social Christian Renovation Party)

NATIONAL HOLIDAYS

January 1	Año Nuevo	New Year's Day
March/April	Semana Santa	Holy Week (Maundy Thursday, Good Friday, Holy Saturday, Easter)
May 1	Día del Trabajo	Day of Work (Labor Day)
August 2–6	Festival de San Salvador	Feast of San Salvador

September 15	Día de la Independencia	Independence Day
October 12	Día de la Raza	Day of the Race (Columbus Day)
November 1	Grito de la Independencia	Cry of Independence Day
November 2	Día de los Muertos	Day of the Dead (All Soul's Day)
December 24	Noche de Navidad	Christmas Eve
December 25	Navidad	Christmas

GUATEMALA

BACKGROUND

Official Name:	Republic of Guatemala
Capital:	Guatemala
Federal Flag:	Three vertical bands of light blue, white, and light blue with the coat of arms centered on the white band
Area:	42,042 sq mi (108,889 sq km)
Highest Point:	Volcán Tajumulco, 13,812 ft (4,211 m)
Lowest Point:	Pacific Ocean (sea level)
Natural Resources:	Petroleum, nickel, wood, fish, chicle
Population (7/1998 est.):	12,007,580
Population Growth (1998 est.):	2.7%
Ethnicity:	56% mestizo (ladino); 44% Indian or predominantly Indian

Language:	Spanish, 23 Indian languages including Quiché, Cakchquel, Kekchi
Literacy:	55.6% (although Spanish is the official language, many indigenous people speak only their own language)
Religions:	Roman Catholic, Protestant, traditional Maya
Currency:	1 quetzal = 100 centavos
Economic Overview:	Agriculture, primarily coffee, accounts for two-thirds of Guatemala's exports and over 50% of employment. Recent programs of economic liberalization have enticed foreign investment, fueling growth and decreasing inflation. Guatemala remains challenged by an unstable monetary policy.
GDP (1997 est.):	$45.8 billion
GDP per Capita (1997 est.):	$4,000
Inflation Rate (1997 est.):	9%
Major Trading Partners:	United States, Central America, Germany, Japan
Unemployment (1997):	5.2%
Employment by Industry:	58% agriculture; 14% services; 14% manufacturing; 7% commerce; 4% construction; 2.6% transport; 0.3% utilities; 0.1% mining

THE LAND AND CLIMATE

Guatemala's topography includes a mountainous central area flanked by a narrow coastline, consisting of mostly black-sand beaches, on the Pacific side, and lowlands and fertile river valleys on the east. In the western highlands there are over 30 volcanoes. El Petén, an expansive jungle lowland, occupies the interior regions. In addition to frequent earthquakes in volcanic areas, Guatemala experiences hurricanes and tropical storms in the Caribbean coastal areas.

Guatemala's climate is as varied as its landscape. The lowlands are typically tropical, while the highlands vary from freezing during the rainy season's nights to warm during the dry season's days. The rainy season lasts from June to October.

THE PEOPLE

Guatemala's population is almost equally divided between ladinos (mestizos), who are of mixed Spanish and Indian heritage, and Maya. Approximately one-third of the population, mostly ladino, is urban. For the two-thirds of the population who live in rural areas, life traditionally revolves around agriculture. Guatemala also has a small population of *gariganu*, Caribbean blacks who are descended from freed slaves.

GUATEMALAN HISTORY IN BRIEF

1000S BC	**One of the earliest known societies is at Las Characas in the Guatemalan highland regions.**
AD 250–900	**The Maya Indian civilization thrives in Guatemala, but abandons its cities c. 900 for unknown reasons.**
1523	**A Spanish expedition led by Pedro de Alvarado**

invades Guatemala. Alvarado defeats all of the Indian groups and establishes Spanish rule in the country.

1570   Spain sets up the Audiencia of Guatemala, a high court of judges and administrators, in what is now Antigua.

1776   The Audiencia is moved to Guatemala City after an earthquake destroys Antigua.

1821   Guatemala gains its independence from Spain and joins the Mexican empire along with the Central American States.

1823   Guatemala and the Central American States break away from the Mexican empire and form the United Provinces of Central America.

1839   The union that was formed as the United Provinces of Central America begins to fall apart; Guatemala leaves the union.

1865   A conservative general, Rafael Carrera, rules as a dictator-president.

1871   The liberals rise to power.

1944   A 10-year period of social and economic revolution begins after protests force dictator Jorge Ubico to resign.

1945   A new constitution is adopted.

1951   Colonel Jacobo Arbenz Guzmán is elected president.

1952   The government begins to take over many privately owned lands and distribute them among the landless peasants.

1954   Rebels attack the Arbenz government from their base in Honduras. The Guatemalan Army refuses to support Arbenz and he is forced to resign.

1956	Guatemala's fifth constitution is adopted.
1963	The army again seizes the government.
1966	The sixth constitution goes into effect.
1970	Violence becomes widespread as various groups of the leftists fight government forces.
1970–82	Guatemala holds four presidential elections; military officers win each time.
1976	A major earthquake strikes Guatemala, causing 23,000 deaths and about $700 million worth of property damage.
1982	General Angel Anibal Guevara wins the presidential election.
1983	Military leaders overthrow Rios Montt.
1985	The people elect Marco Vinicio Cerezo Arevalo, a civilian, president. A new constitution is written, the Congress reestablished, and political party activities are allowed once again.
1991	A new civilian president, Jorge Serrano Elías, is elected.
1993	In May, Serrano dissolves congress and announces that he now rules by presidential order. In June, the military removes Serrano from office and Ramiro de León Carpio replaces him as president.
1996	Voters elect Alvaro Arzu Irgoyen president. The opposition groups and the government sign a peace agreement ending conflict.

POLITICS AND GOVERNMENT

Guatemala has 22 administrative *departamentos* (departments):

ALTA VERAPAZ	CHIMALTENANGO
BAJA VERAPAZ	CHIQUIMULA

EL PETÉN	RETALHULEU
EL PROGRESO	SACATEPÉQUEZ
EL QUICHÉ	SAN MARCOS
ESCUINTLA	SANTA ROSA
GUATEMALA	SOLOLÁ
HUEHUETENANGO	SUCHITEPÉQUEZ
IZABAL	TOTONICAPÁN
JALAPA	ZACAPA
QUETZALTENANGO	JUTIAPA

The chief of state and head of government, the president, who is elected by popular vote to a four-year term, the vice president, and the Council of Ministers make up the executive branch of government.

The legislative branch is comprised of the unicameral *Congreso de la República* (Congress of the Republic), whose 80 members are elected by popular vote to serve four-year terms.

The *Corte Suprema de Justicia* (Supreme Court of Justice), presided over by the president of the Supreme Court, is the judicial branch of government. Supreme Court justices are elected by Congress to five-year terms.

Political Parties

ALIANZA DEMOCRÁTICA (Democratic Alliance)
DEMOCRACIA CRISTIANA GUATEMALTECA—DCG
   (Christian Democratic Party)
FRENTE REPUBLICANO GUATEMALTECO—FRG
   (Guatemalan Republican Front)
PARTIDO DE AVANZADA NACIONAL—PAN (National
   Advancement Party)
PARTIDO LABORISTA GUATEMALTECO—PLG
   (Guatemalan Labor Party)
PARTIDO LIBERTADOR PROGRESISTA—PLP
   (Progresist Party for Liberation)

Union Democrática—UD (Democratic Union)
Union Nacionalista—UN (Nationalist Union)

NATIONAL HOLIDAYS

January 1	Año Nuevo	New Year's Day
March/April	Semana Santa	Holy Week (Maundy Thursday, Good Friday, Holy Saturday, Easter)
May 1	Día del Trabajo	Day of Work (Labor Day)
June 30	Día del Ejértico	Army Day
August 15	Guatemala City Fiesta	
September 15	Día de la Independencia	Independence Day
October 20	Aniversario de la Revolución	Celebration of the Revolution of 1944
November 1	Todos los Santos	All Saint's Day
December 24	Noche de Navidad	Christmas Eve (half day)
December 25	Navidad	Christmas
December 31	Noche del Año Nuevo	New Year's Eve (half day)

HONDURAS

BACKGROUND

Official Name:	República de Honduras (Republic of Honduras)
Capital:	Tegucigalpa
Federal Flag:	Equal horizontal bands of blue, white, and blue with five blue five-pointed stars (representing the five members

of the former Federal Republic of Central America—Costa Rica, El Salvador, Guatemala, Honduras, and Nicaragua) centered on the white band in an X pattern

Area:	43,270 sq mi (112,090 sq km)
Highest Point:	Cerro La Minas, 9,413 ft (2,870 m)
Lowest Point:	Caribbean Sea (sea level)
Natural Resources:	Timber, gold, silver, copper, lead, zinc, iron ore, antimony, coal, fish
Population (7/1998 est.):	5,861,955
Population Growth (1998 est.):	2.33%
Largest Cities:	Tegucigalpa, San Pedro Sula
Ethnicity:	90% mestizo (mixed European and Indian), 7% Native American, 2% black, 1% white
Language:	Spanish, Native American languages
Literacy:	72.7%
Religions:	97% Roman Catholic; Protestant minority
Currency:	1 lempira = 100 centavos
Economic Overview:	Honduras is one of the poorest countries in the western hemisphere; agriculture accounts for almost two-thirds of the labor force and two-thirds of exports. Rapid population growth, high underemployment, inflation, and a lack of basic services are some of the challenges Honduras faces.
GDP (1997 est.):	$12.7 billion

GDP per Capita (1997 est.):	$2,200
Inflation Rate (1997 est.):	17%
Major Trading Partners:	United States, European Union, Guatemala, Japan, Mexico, El Salvador
Unemployment (1997):	6.3% (underemployment is at 30%)
Employment by Industry:	65% agriculture; 20% services; 9% manufacturing; 3% construction; 6% other

THE LAND AND CLIMATE

The Honduran landscape consists of a mountainous interior with a narrow coastal plain area. In the coastal lowlands the climate is subtropical, although the mountains are temperate.

THE PEOPLE

Honduras's population is 90% mestizo, a mixture of Spanish and Native American heritage, and 7% pure Native American, with blacks and whites making up the remaining 3%. The native people tend to be concentrated in small areas and each group has its own language and cultural traditions. More than half of the population lives in rural areas, where poverty, inadequate housing, and sanitation are problems. However, Honduras is seeing a rapid move of its population toward the urban areas, and the balance will probably soon tip in favor of the urban population.

1502	Columbus explores Honduras during his last voyage to the New World.
1524	The conquest of Honduras by Spain begins.
1525	Hernán Cortés arrives in Honduras and establishes a colony.
1821	Honduras declares its independence from Spain and, together with Costa Rica, El Salvador, Guatemala, and Nicaragua, forms the United Provinces of Central America.
1827–29	Francisco Morazán leads liberal forces to victory in a bloody civil war and becomes president of the federation during its last 10 years.
1832	The dictatorship of General Tiburcio Carias Andino begins
1838	Honduras leaves the Federation of Central American States.
1840–1870s	Following Morazán's fall from power, Honduras is ruled by a series of conservative dictatorships, including those of Francisco Ferrera, Juan Lindo, and Santos Guardiola.
1876	Marcos A. Sato, more liberal than his predecessors, although still a dictator, gains power and focuses on modernization and increasing exports.
1957	The liberal Ramón Villeda Morales is elected by a constituent assembly; he leads the country into the Central American Common Market (CACM) and initiates programs for agrarian reform and education.
1963	Ramón Villeda Morales's policies and apprehension over the rise of communism in Cuba set the stage for a coup led by Colonel Osvaldo López Arellano.

1969	A brief but costly war with El Salvador erupts over the issue of Salvadoran immigration to Honduras, further weakening the fragile Honduran economy.
1975	Colonel Juan Alberto Melgar Castro is ousted in a coup led by General Policarpo Paz García.
1980	General Paz signs a peace treaty with El Salvador.
1982	After a decade of military rule, Roberto Suazo Cordova is elected president, although the military retains considerable influence. Honduras faces severe economic challenges and tensions along its border with Nicaragua.
1985	José Azcona Hoyo becomes the first civilian to be elected president.
1995	Honduras joins the Association of Caribbean States (ACS), a free trade organization.
1997	The lack of a resolution to the maritime border dispute with Nicaragua leads to the exchange of fire between Nicaraguan and Honduran ships.
1997	Carlos Flores Facussé of the Liberal Party is elected president.

POLITICS AND GOVERNMENT

Honduras has 18 *departamentos* (departments) plus the Central District of Tegucigalpa. The executive branch of the Honduran government consists of the president, who is head of both the state and the government, the first, second, and third vice presidents and the Cabinet. Presidential elections are held every four years.

The legislature is the unicameral *Asamblea Nacional* (National

Assembly), which has 128 members who are elected to four-year terms. Seats are assigned to the parties' candidates in proportion to the number of votes received by each party in a popular election.

The *Corte Suprema de Justica* (Supreme Court of Justice) forms the judicial branch; its judges are elected to four-year terms by the *Asamblea Nacional.*

Departamentos

ATLÁNTIDA	INTIBUCÁ
CHOLUTECA	ISLAS DE LA BAHÍA
COLÓN	LA PAZ
COMAYAGUA	LEMPIRA
COPÁN	OCOTEPEQUE
CORTÉS	OLANCHO
EL PARAÍSO	SANTA BARBARA
FRANCISCO MORAZÁN	VALLE
GRACIAS DIOS	YORO

Political Parties

PARTIDO DEMÓCRATA CRISTIANO—PDC
   (Christian Democratic Party)
PARTIDO INNOVACIÓN Y UNIDAD—PINU
   (National Innovation and Unity Party)
PARTIDO LIBERAL—PL (Liberal Party)
PARTIDO NACIONAL—PN (National Party)

NATIONAL HOLIDAYS

January 1	Año Nuevo	New Year's Day
March/April	Semana Santa	Holy Week (Maundy Thursday, Good Friday, Holy Saturday, Easter)
April 14	Día de las Americas	Day of the Americas

May 1	Día del Trabajo	Day of Work (Labor Day)
September 15	Día de la Independencia	Independence Day
October 3	Francisco Morazán Day	
October 12	Día de la Raza	Day of the Race (Columbus Day)
October 21	Armed Forces Day	
December 24	Noche Buena	Christmas Eve (half day)
December 25	Navidad	Christmas
December 31	Año Nuevo	New Year's Eve (half day)

Festivals and Celebrations

In addition to national holidays, Hondurans celebrate a host of religious, regional, and local holidays and festivals. Like most of Central America, many cities and towns have a patron saint, such as the Virgin of Suyapa in Tegucigalpa, whom they honor with a fiesta on the appropriate day.

NICARAGUA

BACKGROUND

Official Name:	Republic of Nicaragua
Capital:	Managua
Federal Flag:	Three equal horizontal stripes of blue, white and blue with the national coat of arms centered on the white band

Area	50,464 sq mi (130,700 sq km)
Highest Point:	Mogoton, 7,996 ft (2,438 m)
Lowest Point:	Pacific Ocean (sea level)
Natural Resources:	Gold, silver, copper, tungsten, lead, zinc, timber, fish
Population (7/1998 est.):	4,583,379
Population Growth (1998 est.):	2.92%
Largest Cities:	Managua, León, Granada, Jinotega
Ethnicity:	69% mestizo; 17% white; 9% black; 5% Native American
Language:	Spanish (English- and Indian language–speaking minorities)
Literacy:	65.7%
Religions:	95% Roman Catholic, 5% Protestant
Currency:	1 gold cordoba = 100 centavos
Economic Overview:	Nicaragua's economy has bounced back following economic disaster in the 1980s caused by economic misman-agement and civil war. Economic growth has risen and inflation has been reduced. The Nicaraguan economy is based primarily on agriculture, but the rapidly expanded tourism industry has become the country's third-largest industry.
GDP (1997 est.):	$9.3 billion
GDP per Capita (1997 est.):	$2,100

Inflation Rate (1997 est.):	11.6%
Major Trading Partners:	United States, Central America, Germany, Venezuela, Japan, Canada
Unemployment (1997):	16%
Employment by Industry:	54% services; 31% agriculture; 15% industry

THE LAND AND CLIMATE

The Atlantic coastal plains extend to central mountains and descend again to a narrow Pacific coastal plain spotted with volcanoes. The climate, while cooler in the highlands, is tropical in the lowlands. Earthquakes, volcanoes, landslides, and hurricanes are among the threats of nature that Nicaraguans sometimes endure.

THE PEOPLE

The majority of Nicaraguans are descended from both European and indigenous ancestors. The native and black (of Jamaican descent) populations are concentrated in the eastern part of the country. In 1995 the government divided the department of Zelaya on the Atlantic cost into two autonomous regions, Atlántico Norte and Atlántico Sur, granting people in those regions limited self-rule. Reforms to the constitution in 1995 guarantee that cultures can retain their customs and languages.

1524	Hernández de Córdoba founds the first permanent Spanish settlements.
1821	Nicaragua gains its independence from Spain and briefly becomes part of the Mexican Empire before joining other countries to form the United Provinces of Central America.
1838	Nicaragua breaks from the Central American federation to become an independent republic.
1856	William Walker, an American, seizes the presidency after joining the liberals in their struggle against the conservatives; he is driven from office by the joint effort of the liberals and conservatives in 1857, beginning three decades of conservative rule.
1893	José Santos Zelaya, taking advantage of internal conservative divisiveness, leads a liberal revolt that brings him into power.
1909	A new conservative government is established.
1912–33	The United States sends a detachment of Marines to Nicaragua to support the new conservative government.
1927–33	U.S. Marines engage in an ongoing battle with rebel forces led by liberal guerrilla leader General César Augusto Sandino.
1916	The Bryan-Chamoro Treaty gives the United States an option to build a canal through Nicaragua and to establish naval bases.
1936–56	General Anastasio Somoza García emerges and rules as a dictator until his assassination; his two sons succeed him.
1979	Somoza rule ends as Sandinista guerrillas, leftists who took their name from General Sandino, launch an offensive. Sandinistas

assume power, promising to maintain a mixed economy, a non-aligned foreign policy, and a pluralist political system.

1981   The United States suspends U.S. aid, charging that Nicaragua, with the aid of Cuba and the Soviet Union, is supplying arms to rebels in El Salvador. Nicaraguan guerrillas known as Contras begin a war to overthrow the Sandinistas.

1984   Elections are held and Daniel Ortega Saavedra, the Sandinista junta coordinator, wins the presidency.

1986–87   The war between the Contras and the Sandinistas intensifies as the resupplied Contras establish themselves inside the country.

1990s   Elections end 11 years of Sandinista rule.

1991   President Chamorro brings the military under her command.

1993   Relations between President Chamorro and the coalition that backed her sour over charges of corruption and the continuing influence of the Sandinistas in the government and the army.

1996   Arnoldo Alemán, a former Managua mayor and conservative candidate, wins the presidential election.

POLITICS AND GOVERNMENT

Nicaragua has 15 *departamentos* (departments), and two *regiones autonomistas* (autonomous regions).

Departamentos

BOACO	MADRIZ
CARAZO	MANAGUA
CHINANDEGA	MASAYA
CHONTALES	MATAGALPA
ESTELÍ	NUEVA SEGOVIA
GRANADA	RÍO SAN JUAN
JINOTEGA	RIVAS
LEÓN	

Regiones Autonomistas

ATLÁNTICO NORTE
ATLÁNTICO SUR

The government is divided into executive, legislative, judicial, and electoral branches. The executive branch consists of the president, who is elected by popular vote to a five-year term, the vice president, and the Cabinet.

The unicameral *Asamblea Nacional* (National Assembly) performs legislative functions and consists of 93 seats. Its members are elected by proportional representation to five-year terms. The 1995 reform of the 1987 Sandinista constitution gave the *Asamblea Nacional* the ability to override a presidential veto with a simple majority and weakened the president's ability to veto a bill.

The *Corte Suprema* (Supreme Court), the judicial branch, consists of twelve justices who are elected to seven-year terms by the *Asamblea Nacional*.

The Supreme Electoral Council, led by a council of five magistrates, is responsible for organizing and conducting elections, plebiscites, and referendums. It is a co-equal branch of the government and its members are elected by the *Assamblea Nacional* to five-year terms.

Political Parties

Nicaragua has some 35 political parties that frequently form alliances to gain voting power. Parties that do not win at least one seat in the *Assamblea Nacional* automatically lose their legal status. The following are some of the major parties:

CONSERVATIVE ACTION MOVEMENT—MAC

CONSERVATIVE PARTY OF NICARAGUA—PCN

INDEPENDENT LIBERAL PARTY—PLI

INDEPENDENT LIBERAL PARTY FOR
    NATIONAL UNITY—PLIUN

LIBERAL CONSTITUTIONALIST PARTY—PLC

NATIONAL CONSERVATIVE PARTY—PCN

NATIONAL DEMOCRATIC PARTY—PUCA

NATIONALIST LIBERAL PARTY—PLN

NATIONAL PROJECT—PRONAL

NEOLIBERAL PARTY—PALI

NICARAGUAN DEMOCRATIC MOVEMENT—MDN

NICARAGUAN PARTY OF THE CHRISTIAN ROAD—PCCN

NICARAGUAN RESISTANCE PARTY—PRN

SANDINISTA NATIONAL LIBERATION FRONT—FSLN

SANDINISTA RENOVATION MOVEMENT—MRS

SOCIAL CHRISTIAN PARTY—PSC

SOCIAL DEMOCRATIC PARTY—PSD

UNITY ALLIANCE—AU

UNO-96 ALLIANCE

NATIONAL HOLIDAYS

January 1	Año Nuevo	New Year's Day
March/April	Jueves Santo	Holy Thursday
March/April	Viernes Santo	Good Friday
May 1	Día del Trabajo	Labor Day
July 19	El Triunfo	Triumph of the Revolution of 1979
September 14	Batalla de San Jacinto	Battle of San Jacinto
September 15	Día de la Independencia	Independence Day
September 24	Matagalpa, Virgin de la Merced	Our Lady of Mercy
October 12	Día de la Raza	Columbus Day
November 2	Día de los Fieles Difuntos	Day of the Dead
December 8	La Immaculada Concepción	Immaculate Conception
December 24-25	Navidad	Christmas Eve and Christmas

PANAMA

BACKGROUND

Official Name: Republic of Panama

Capital: Panama

Federal Flag: Four equal rectangles; the top rectangles are white, with a blue five-pointed star in the center, and red; the bottom rectangles are blue and white with a red five-pointed in the center.

Area: 29,157 sq mi (75,517 sq km)

Highest Point: Volcán de Chiriquí, 11,398 ft (3,475 m)

Lowest Point:	Pacific Ocean (sea level)
Natural Resources:	Copper, mahogany forests, shrimp
Population (7/1998 est.):	2,735,943
Population Growth (1998 est.):	1.56%
Largest Cities:	Panama City, Colón
Ethnicity:	70% mestizo; 14% black or West Indian; 10% white; 6% Native American
Language:	Spanish (official), English
Literacy:	90.8%
Religions:	85% Roman Catholic; 15% Protestant
Currency:	1 balboa = 100 centesimos
Economic Overview:	Panama's economy is service-based, including banking, commerce, and tourism. Reforms in recent years have liberalized trade, privatized state-owned enterprises, and encouraged foreign investment and job creation. The Panama Canal, shipping, and port activities have helped drive GDP growth.
GDP (1997 est.):	$18 billion
GDP per Capita (1997 est.):	$6,700
Inflation Rate (1997 est.):	1.2%
Major Trading Partners:	United States, European Union, Central America, and the Caribbean
Unemployment (1997):	13.1%

Employment by Industry:	31.8% government and community services; 26.8% agriculture, hunting, fishing; 16.4% commerce, restaurants, hospitality; 9.4% manufacturing and mining; 6.2% transportation and communications; 4.3% finance, insurance, real estate

THE LAND AND CLIMATE

The central highlands are mountainous, with the Tabasara Mountains extending eastward from the Costa Rican border. The San Blas and Darien mountains lie near the Panama Canal. The valleys in western Panama are very fertile farming land.

The coastal lowlands are narrow areas along the Panama's Pacific and Atlantic Coasts. In the west, the Pacific lowlands have fertile land for farming; farming in the Atlantic lowlands is less favorable.

There are about 800 islands near Panama's coast, all part of the country's territory. The largest islands, found off the Pacific coast, are Coiba Island and Rey Island.

Panama has a tropical climate with an extended rainy season lasting from May to January.

THE PEOPLE

Panama has one of Central America's smallest populations, with most of the population living in the urban corridor between Panama City and Colón, Panama's biggest cities.

Panama's population is made up of a rich mix of ethnic heritages, including mestizos, whites, blacks of African descent, and indigenous tribes. Mestizos, who make up over two-thirds of the population, trace their roots to any combination of Spaniards, slaves brought to the area in colonial times, and Native Americans. Blacks descend from African slaves and West Indian (called *antillanos*) workers who immigrated to Panama to work on the Canal in the early 1900s; together they make up 14% of the population, Panama's largest minority. The native population includes the Kuna, Guaym, Emberá, and Choc tribes.

PANAMA HISTORY IN BRIEF

1500s	Panama is inhabited by over 60 native tribes, including the Maya and the Chibchas.
1501	Rodrigo de Bastidas, a Spanish explorer, is the first white person to reach the area.
1502	Columbus visits Panama on his fourth voyage.
1510	A group of Spanish soldiers and colonists settles in Panama.
1513	Vasco Nuñez de Balboa explores Panama.
1530s	Spaniards, led by Francisco Pizarro, conquer the Peruvian Incas.
1600s	English pirate Henry Morgan and other pirates attack Spanish ships and towns in Panama.
1821	Central America revolts against Spain, and Panama declares its independence and becomes a province of Colombia.
1830	Panamanians revolt against Colombia.
1850–1900s	A volatile period with 40 administrations, 50 riots, 5 attempted secessions, and 13 U.S. interventions.
1855	The railroad is completed by businessmen from the United States to speed up passage across the

isthmus; Panama becomes a busy transportation hub.

1903	Colombia refuses an offer by the United States to build a canal across Panama. Panama proclaims its independence from Colombia, backed by the United States. The Hay-Buneau-Varilla Treaty between Panama and the United States grants the United States the right to construct a canal through the Isthmus of Panama.
1914	The Panama Canal opens on August 15.
1933	U.S. payment for rights to the Panama Canal increases from $250,000 a year to $430,000 a year.
1955	The annual fee for Canal access increases even more under a revised treaty.
1968	Omar Torrijos Herrera, a military officer, takes control of Panama as dictator.
1974	Panama and the United States agree to negotiate the eventual reversion of the Canal to Panama despite opposition by the U.S. Congress.
1977	The Panama Canal Treaty between Panama and the United States brings the Canal under a joint Canal Commission until December 31, 1999, at which time it was turned over to the government of Panama.
1978	General Torrijos gives up control of Panama's government.
1979	A treaty results in the transfer of the Canal Zone to Panama.
1981	General Torrijos dies in a plane crash.
1983	General Manuel Antonio Noriega becomes head of the military and Panama's most powerful leader.
1984	Nicolas Ardito Barletta, Panama's first directly

elected president in 16 years but a puppet of Noriega, is inaugurated.

1987   A former aide of Noriega accuses him of election fraud.

1988   Noriega is indicted in the United States for drug trafficking.

1989   The National Assembly names Noriega the maximum leader and declares war on the United States. An attempt by Panamanian soldiers to overthrow Noriega fails. U.S. troops seize control of Panama City as they attempt to capture Noriega.

1990   Noriega surrenders himself to U.S. custody and is transported to Miami to stand trial.

1992   Noriega is convicted for trafficking drugs.

1994   Ernesto Pérez of the Democratic Revolutionary Party wins the election as president.

1997   A new law creates an autonomous Canal Authority to administer the Panama Canal after the United States relinquishes control over the waterway.

POLITICS AND GOVERNMENT

Panama is a constitutional republic with nine *provincias* (provinces) and two *comarca* (territories).*

Provincias

BOCAS DEL TORO   COCLÉ
CHIRIQUÍ   COLÓN

*One new, as yet unnamed, territory was created in March 1997.

HERRERA	PANAMÁ
LOS SANTOS	SAN BLAS (territory)
DARIÉN	VERAGUAS

The executive branch of government includes the president, who is elected by direct popular vote to a five-year term, and the first and second vice presidents. The vice presidents are elected on the same ticket as the president.

The legislative branch is the unicameral *Asamblea Legislative*, with 72 members who are elected by popular vote to five-year terms.

The judicial branch consists of the *Corte Suprema de Justicia* (Supreme Court of Justice), five superior courts and three courts of appeal. Supreme Court justices are appointed to 10-year terms.

Political Parties

PARTIDO REVOLUCIONARIO DEMOCRÁTICO—PRD
   (DEMOCRATIC REVOLUTIONARY PARTY)
PARTIDO LIBERAL NACIONAL—PLN
   (NATIONAL LIBERAL PARTY)
PARTIDO SOLARIDAD—PS
MOVIMIENTO LIBERAL REPUBLICANO
   NACIONALISTA—MOLIRENA (NATIONALIST
   REPUBLICAN LIBERAL MOVEMENT)
PARTIDO ARNULFISTA—PA (ARNULFISTA PARTY)
PARTIDO DEMÓCRATA CRISTIANO—PDC
   (CHRISTIAN DEMOCRATIC PARTY)
PARTIDO LABORISTA—PALA (LABOR PARTY)

NATIONAL HOLIDAYS

January 1	Año Nuevo	New Year's Day
January 9	Día de los Mártires	Martyrs' Day (Day of Mourning)
February/March	Martes de Carnaval	Carnival Tuesday
March/April	Viernes Santo	Good Friday

May 1	Día del Trabajo	Day of Work (Labor Day)
November 3	Día de la Independencia	Independence Day (from Colombia)
November 10	Día de Todos los Santos	Uprising of Los Santos
November 28	Día de la Independencia	Independence Day (from Spain)
December 8	Día de la Madre	Mother's Day
December 25	Navidad	Christmas

CULTURE

We all have programmed into us a certain code, a set of rules by which we live. These rules govern our actions, and our reactions. They are instilled in us by our parents, our teachers, and our peers. Culture, then, is the combined values, beliefs, mores, motivations, and attitudes that shape our view of the world.

Though we are all individuals, we are influenced by the culture in which we grew up. Despite our individual differences, there are nevertheless cultural ties that bind us together. No matter how little someone from Des Moines thinks he has in common with a New Yorker, they are indeed more like each other than like someone from Tokyo or Riyadh.

This chapter explores the cultural differences between Central America and the United States. Although endless distinctions can be made between cultures, here we break culture down into six different categories that will paint a practical, accessible portrait of Central American culture viewed through American eyes. These categories are: time, communication, relationships, status/hierarchy, group dynamics, and reasoning style. Each section begins a brief overview of the category and the polar opposites. As we explore the category in more depth, we will take a look at where the Central American countries and the United States fall on the continuum and how they relate to each other. By the end of the section, you should have a greater understanding of what may cause cultural misunderstanding and an idea of the very real challenges communicating across cultures can present. Finally, we will provide you with some tips to help you apply this information to your daily interactions with Central Americans. We will use this knowledge as we take a step-by-step look at Central American business culture in later chapters.

With any luck, you will emerge with a better understanding not only of what makes Central Americans tick, but of what makes you tick as well. Only when you are able to understand that cultural differences are neither bad nor good, merely different ways to look at the same reality, can you begin to build the cross-cultural skills you will need to be successful in Central America—or anywhere else in the world.

The following observations are of necessity painted in broad strokes. It is naturally unwise to think that every Central American will behave in one way and every American in another. However, there is enough evidence to support the idea that Central Americans as a culture tend to have certain preferences, as do Americans.

Keeping that in mind, the information in this chapter will give you a foundation on which to lay the bricks of individual characteristics, quirks and foibles.

TIME

No por mucho madrugar,
amanece más temprano.

The sun doesn't rise any earlier
just because you get up earlier.

Steve Riley was growing more and more frustrated as his one-week trip to Central America wound down. There was no way he was going to be able to accomplish all that he had planned during his visits to his company's three offices in Mexico and Panama. People seemed determined to disrupt his schedule. It seemed that every time he arrived for an appointment he was kept waiting, every meeting started late and dragged on well past the ending time he had planned. He ended up spending late evenings in his hotel room just trying to make up for the time that had been wasted during the day. Now it looked like he was going to have to make a second trip down and wondered when he'd be able to squeeze that in before the end of the quarter.

Rigid Versus Flexible Cultures

Perhaps the first cultural challenge people encounter, often subconsciously, when they meet another culture is differences in the perception of time. Time is a resource that different cultures view differently. We all have different answers to the questions "What is the value of time?" and "How is time best spent?" In the most basic terms, time can be either flexible or rigid.

In a rigid-time culture, the clock is the measure against which all of our actions are judged: whether we are saving time or wasting it, whether we are on time or late. People in rigid-time cultures like to plan their activities and keep a schedule. It is rude to show up late and important not to waste other people's time. Time is a commodity that must be spent wisely, not frittered away.

The clock for flexible-time cultures is more fluid, and things can happen more spontaneously. Plans are made, but with the understanding that they may be changed, even at the last minute, depending on circumstances. Punctuality is not a virtue, and many things can take precedence over adherence to a schedule.

Central American–American Interaction

The difference in the way we view time is the most readily noticeable—and the most commented upon—cultural conflict between

Americans and Central Americans. While neither culture is at the farthest reaches of the time continuum, there is a substantial gap between the importance each culture places on time, as well as in how time is best spent.

Americans in general find themselves ruled by the clock. Time is a limited asset that Americans schedule carefully and often fully. The American businessperson's accessories are incomplete without an ever-present daily planner, which is divided into half-hour or even fifteen-minute increments in order to allow close scheduling. With such tight scheduling, people inevitably run late, but extreme or frequent tardiness is discourteous and will at best irritate the people whom you have inconvenienced. Deadlines in the United States are serious business.

Central Americans tend to have a much more relaxed approach to time. Appointments and schedules act more as guidelines, and it's understood that other things are more important than paying obeisance to the clock. If, for instance, a Central American is speaking with a colleague in his office, he won't cut him short or rush him off simply because it is time for another appointment. An American in the same situation would probably prefer to schedule another meeting with his colleague to continue the discussion at a later date so that he can keep his scheduled appointment.

By the same token, a missed or delayed deadline (which is after all only a target) is neither a crisis nor a reason to panic in Central America. It is merely a change in plans, and, as past experience has shown, all will most likely work out in the end.

The Central American's relaxed attitude toward time is often a source of great frustration to Americans, whose anxiety level increases when things don't go as planned. This can be exacerbated if the Central American, for whom a delay is not outside of the norm, does not inform the American. This can lead to strained relations as the Central American begins to feel that the American is too impatient and is pressuring him too hard, while the American suspects the competence and dedication of a person who cannot be bothered to even let his colleagues know if a project falls behind schedule.

Tips on Time

- Accept the fact that your view of time is probably different from your Central American colleague's. With that in mind, you may find it helpful to build in a cushion for potential delays. This can be helpful in planning, especially if you are reporting to management that has a more rigid view of time to ensure that expectations are kept realistic.
- Keep the lines of communication open. Communicate your needs and, if you are a manager, help your subordinates prioritize tasks. Just explaining why you need something done on a certain timeline can go a long way in getting it done.
- Try to communicate to your subordinates and colleagues your need to know when there will be delays. They may be inclined to tell you what you want to hear, but are more likely to keep you abreast of delays if you demonstrate that you just want to be kept up to date, not to punish anyone.
- Nurture your flexibility and patience skills. There is really nothing you can do to change people when it comes to the way they think. Relax and enjoy the pace of life as much as possible.

COMMUNICATION

Una palabra hiere más que una cuchillada.
A word can hurt more than a stabbing.

Luis Blanco's supervisor, Julie Anderson, called him into her office to discuss his performance. Luis was astonished to learn that Julie felt he wasn't being a team player. She cited as evidence a recent project that Luis had been working on. There had been some problems that had delayed the launch of the company's new software program. Julie wanted to know why Luis had reported several times that everything was on track when obviously it wasn't. Why hadn't Luis let Julie know that there was a problem as soon as it happened?

Direct versus Indirect Communication

What is the goal of communication? Regardless of what culture you are from, you need to be able to relay information to other people. But is that the goal in and of itself, or are there other variables that affect the goal?

In cultures that value direct communication, the goal of communication is mainly to relay information. Value is placed on being able to state your point in a clear and concise manner, and words have limited nuances. In general, people do not appreciate having to pull the real point out from a surfeit of words.

If you are an indirect communicator, on the other hand, you have to take other factors into account. It may be important not to cause offense to your listener, to show deference, or to maintain harmony, for example. Very often the real meaning in indirect communication cultures is a subtext buried under many layers of meaning or intertwined with non-verbal clues or metaphor.

Central American–American Interaction

"Just get to the point," says the American. In the United States, a direct approach to communication is the preference. It is a point of pride to be able to state your case clearly and succinctly. While Americans aren't the robotic creatures that implies, there is definitely a value placed on explicit and concise communication, especially in business. The successful speaker at a conference is one who follows the golden rule of public speaking: Keep It Short and Simple, known as KISS. The speaker who flops is the one meandering around his topic, causing people to fidget and glance at their watches.

Certainly in American interactions there is room for recognizing the feelings of the other person, but there is an expectation that one is able to separate criticism of one's actions from criticism of one's self. In reality, that is often not so easy, and as a consequence, many Americans resort to the tactic of leading into criticism with praise. An American in the position of having to tell a subordinate that she is in jeopardy of being fired if she continues to be late to work will probably first reassure her of her value to the company, following up with the infamous "but." "But if you continue to be late, we will be forced to let you go."

In Central America, a more indirect approach is generally favored. "Getting to the point" isn't an immediate goal. More value is placed on a personal connection, so it's important to spend time strengthening that bond. If you are new acquaintances, this may take the form of an extended conversation on general topics before "the point" is reached that will allow each person to get to know the other and begin to build a mutual trust. If you have an established relationship, each person will want to inquire after the other person's well-being and family and otherwise catch up.

The indirect approach can continue into a conversation even when critical topics are (finally, for the American) under discussion. Americans tend to find Central American speech patterns flowery and embellished. For the plain-speaking American, this can be misinterpreted as an attempt to evade or obscure valuable information.

Tips on Communication

- Expect a more indirect communication style and try to modify your style accordingly.
- Communicate respect. Use titles and last names until or unless invited to be more informal.
- Remember that Central Americans don't like to say "no" outright or give bad news. Learn to read between the lines and to interpret both verbal and non-verbal cues. For example, "We would like to do it" is a far cry from "We *will* do it."

GROUP DYNAMICS

Judy Butler was excited to join the team that was negotiating a telecommunications joint venture with a Mexican company. Now on her first trip to Mexico, Judy feels that things are going quite well, but she has to admit that she is tired of the Mexicans' eternal nosiness. People she barely knows feel free to ask her very personal questions. Is she married? Is she engaged? Does she have a boyfriend? In turn, Judy has to listen to tales of the son who is studying in the United States, the daughter who is having a baby soon, even the grandchildren. In short, she is hearing a lot more about her Mexican counterparts than she ever wanted to know.

Group-Oriented Versus Individualistic

In the overall scheme of things, which is stronger: the needs of the individual or the needs of the group? Is it usually the case that indi-

viduals are willing to make sacrifices for the good of the group, or will the group suffer for the benefit of the individual?

We are all faced at one time or another with making a decision to place someone else's needs before our own—our family, our friends, our team at work. Where the deeper cultural differences lie, however, is in the expectations of society. What is the societal norm for looking out for oneself or one's group? The next time you stay late at the office, think about your motives for doing so. Are you really staying to finish the project because it will be an enormous benefit to your company? Or are you staying because in order to advance up the ladder of success it is important that you be perceived as dedicated and hard-working?

Groups can take on many forms. Your group might consist of your family (immediate or extended), co-workers, the company you work for, friends with whom you grew up and went to school, a tribe or clan, a religious group, or a local, regional, or national affiliation. And of course you may belong to many different groups throughout your life.

If you are group-oriented, the group is an inherent part of your identity. You are first and foremost Japanese or a Muslim or Bantu or a member of the Fuentes family, and a major factor in your decisions and actions is how they affect other members of your group. As an individual you are much more inclined to align your own goals with those of the group. Your talent is part of a larger pool, and when you cooperate with others it becomes possible to reach a mutual goal.

Let's look at an example from a hypothetical workplace. Some of the sales people in a particular division brought in more revenue and some less. However, the important thing is that the sales goals were met collectively, so everyone should share equally in the annual bonus according to group-oriented thinking. In this way, individual weaknesses are balanced by others' strengths so that equilibrium is achieved. The success of the team strengthens it and encourages people to strive for higher goals.

The sales scenario wherein everyone shares equally in the bonus when some people have brought in more business than others seems unfair in individualistic cultures. Individualistic people may think, sure, it's great that we met our sales goal, but since I was responsible for more revenue than the other members of the team, I should receive a proportionately larger share of the annual bonus. The fear is that if everyone gets an equal share of the bonus, people are tempted to coast along and not put maximum effort into their jobs. As a member of an individualistic culture, it is important that everyone receive the recognition due him or her, and, conversely, that everyone take responsibility for his or her mistakes.

A culture's inclination toward the group or the individual will be an important influence in areas such as teamwork, rewards and motivation, and decision-making.

Central American–American Interaction

The family is the most important group to most Central Americans. *Familia* for Central Americans is a much broader concept than "family" is for Americans. When an American refers to his or her family, it usually means the nuclear family of mother, father, and children. When one marries and has children of one's own, the nucleus of the family shifts from one's parents to one's children. *Familia*, however, means all generations of the family and extends to in-laws, cousins, aunts, and uncles. It even includes non-family members, such as godparents and the friends of one's parents, who are "adopted" by the use of an honorary *tía* (aunt) or *tío* (uncle). Family takes precedence over most things. Family emergencies, ceremonies, and celebrations (funerals, weddings, etc.) warrant a day off from work when they fall on a weekday.

Families, while important in the United States, tend to be limited to the immediate, nuclear family. Americans usually feel less bound to their families, and most young adults think nothing of moving far away from their parents. Most people, in fact, base their decision to move on career issues rather than on family, and people are generally very mobile. Friendships, as well, are generally more transient. In Central America, one's ties to family and friends are more likely to keep one close to home.

Your identity in Mexico, then, is tied to who you are, unlike in the United States, where you generally identify yourself and others by what you or they do. I would introduce my friend Sergio Vásquez in Central America as the cousin of Manuel García (whom the other person knows) and in America as Sergio, who is a lawyer.

Another aspect of group vs. individual is a reluctance on the part of Central Americans to compete with their colleagues. In the United States it's common for there to be a rivalry—friendly or otherwise—between co-workers, and the one who bests the other is usually rewarded with advancement. The structure of the typical Central American organization precludes much advancement on the basis of merit alone, and the nature of the Central American culture is to prefer harmony over conflict.

Tips on Working with Groups and Individuals

- Accept the fact that your Central American colleagues may have different priorities than you do. Take these differences into account when it comes to evaluating your views on things like working late, taking days off for personal event, and the things that motivate your employees.

- Become part of the group. In many organizations there is more of a personal relationship between colleagues than in the United States. Open yourself up to fitting in.

- Do not push competition on your subordinates or colleagues. Central Americans are largely uncomfortable with competition and prefer to co-exist in harmony. Find other ways to reward and encourage growth and advancement.

STATUS AND HIERARCHY

Teresa López was having a difficult time adjusting to her new expatriate assignment as the regional manager of her company's U.S./Canada region. She had worked hard for her success at home and was disappointed that things just weren't working out in the regional office in Los Angeles. The American staff, who had been so friendly at first, seemed to draw back, leaving her feeling isolated. She didn't understand what was happening, since she was doing her best to be an effective manager. She was devastated when she overheard two of her subordinates saying that she apparently thought she was better than they were. After all, she never participated in their dress down days or joined them for a drink after work. Just who did

Teresa think she was, acting so superior, asked one woman indig-nantly.

Ascribed Versus Achieved Status

Social strata are inherent in all cultures. How we differ is in the way that we gain and attribute status. Do we acquire status by virtue of who we are or by what we do?

Status can be based on the inherent characteristics of a person, over which we have no control, such as age, race, gender, or family background. Or it may be based on what a person has accomplished, including educational and professional qualifications, such as the school one attended or whether one is a sign painter or a doctor.

Certainly when we evaluate other people we use a mixture of these criteria. However, a culture will generally value one over the other. In an ascribed status culture, for example, an employee must show competence in order to advance in his or her job; however, he or she must also have seniority. The wisdom and experience that come with age are valued. Similarly, a manager might be influenced in his or her hiring decisions by the applicant's family background or social connections—or lack thereof. Social strata are generally well-defined and one does not easily move between them.

It is much more common in achieved status cultures to accord status based on accomplishments. Social strata are less defined and it is not uncommon to move up the social ladder. While there are certain benefits that come with seniority, it is certainly possible for younger employees to be promoted above their elders. A person's past and, perhaps more importantly, future performance is valued above age. Many U.S. companies, in fact, have a certain number of "fast track" employees who are expected to move up quickly through the ranks based on their potential performance.

Vertical Versus Lateral Hierarchy

Another aspect of status is whether the hierarchical structure is vertical or lateral. Hierarchy is something that exists in all cultures, whether hidden or overt.

In a vertical hierarchy, the structure tends to be overt. Positions within the hierarchy, corporate or social, are clearly outlined, and it is expected that people show and receive the respect due to them as a result of their position within the hierarchy. This respect is shown in many ways, from the use of titles to the depth of one's bow to the vocabulary one uses. The expatriate manager who tries to get his subordinates to call him "Dave" in a vertical hierarchy probably isn't going to have much luck—his employees will feel uncomfortable using such a disrespectfully familiar form of address to their boss. The title "Mr. Dave" may be the closest his subordinates come to using his first name.

Lateral hierarchies allow more equality among colleagues. Each person must be respected for his or her ability, regardless of position in the company. The more egalitarian nature of lateral hierarchies usually means a more informal environment. Lateral hierarchies also allow for greater empowerment at lower levels, as most decisions related to their jobs are made by employees themselves; there is less direct instruction from superiors. There is less concern for following the exact lines of authority than there is for finding the person who is in a position to take care of the issue at hand. Therefore, an employee who needs information from someone in another part of the business would have the freedom to approach that person directly, rather than channeling the request up through his boss, then on to the other person's boss, and finally down to the person who has the information, a restriction that an employee in a hierarchical organization would find difficult to circumvent.

You will find that a culture's views of the nature and importance of status influence business in the relationship and interaction between superiors and subordinates, in the way that information flows (or does not flow) between individuals, in the decision-making process, and in how people move up through the ranks, to name but a few.

Central American–American Interaction

Most Latin cultures, including Central America's, are more status-conscious and hierarchical than the United States. This can have a great impact, both socially and in business. For example, one immediately notices that people in Central America use last names and titles much more than Americans do. Social status in Central America is indicated by many things, including one's car and house, whether one has household help, how one dresses, and how one comports oneself. This applies in the United States as well, but not to the same extent. For example, if an American company has an outing for its employees, the upper-level managers are expected to blend in with the employees; they will wear casual clothing, play volleyball, and so on. In Central America, however, this is much less likely to happen. Upper-level managers are more inclined to preside over the events; both the employees and the managers might feel uncomfortable mingling on an equal footing.

Organizations tend to have very distinct divisions between levels of authority, and decisions come from the top down. In an American organization, although there is a hierarchy, employees have a greater ability to navigate their way through levels in order to get things done. Ideas can be generated at the lower levels and rise to the top. Because of these differences, Americans find themselves frustrated at the bureaucracy in Central America, often feeling like they can't get things done because no one can or wants to perform tasks outside of limited areas of responsibility; this means that many people must be consulted before a decision can be made and action taken.

Tips on Status and Hierarchy

- Work within the hierarchy; don't try to fight it. It may take longer to accomplish a given task, but remember that you could potentially destroy relationships if you fail to respect the hierarchy.
- If you are a manager, it is likely that your subordinates will expect an authoritarian management style, where you assign tasks but retain responsibility. If you wish to delegate responsibility down, take the long-term approach. Your subordinates may be open to the ideas, but are unlikely to change gears overnight.
- Because Central American countries tend to evaluate status based on who you are and not what you have accomplished,

you may find that you cannot rely on your accomplishments to speak for themselves. Do not hesitate to establish your credibility by way of your company title, the degree you hold, the school you attended, and so on.

RELATIONSHIPS

Greg Walker learned a hard lesson about Mexico during the recession in the mid-'90s. When he started expanding his sales into Mexico in the early '90s, he had worked hard to build his clientele, making trips across the border to visit clients. He prided himself on the fact that he knew the needs of each of his clients—mostly small businesses—as well as he knew his own. However, as his business began to expand, he found he no longer had time to meet one-on-one with his clients. He managed to maintain contact with some of his original clients, but the vast majority were just names on invoices. Many invoices weren't paid when the devaluation crisis hit because many companies

didn't have enough money to pay their bills. Looking back, Greg realized that every one of the clients he knew personally paid their bills, even if they weren't always on time. The losses he wrote off were the sales to companies with whom his company had no personal relationship.

Relationship-Oriented Versus Task-Oriented

In the business of life, what takes the priority: your personal relationships or the tasks you do? If you are from a relationship-oriented culture, relationships come before tasks, and, in fact, may be necessary in order to perform tasks. This can have many implications. A sickness in the family (even the extended family) may take precedence over work; a chance meeting with a friend might delay a scheduled meeting; a deal might not be struck until both parties have had time to build a basis of mutual respect and trust. Relationships—ones that go beyond just working together—are the cornerstones of a life of interdependent networks and are a goal in and of themselves.

Task-oriented folks, on the other hand, tend to focus on the job at hand and leave the relationships to whatever time is left over after the work is finished. No friendship or personal intimacy is necessary to perform one's job, and it is generally considered more professional not to let one's personal life intrude on one's work. The general rule is that one should get on with one's business and worry about "being friends" later.

This is not to say that relationship-builders don't get things done; nor is it meant to imply that task-focused people are not friendly. It simply means that the expectations one has in one's personal and business relationships might not be the same as what is expected in another culture. If you are doing business abroad, you will find that these differences can be crucial to your success. You will see them crop up in negotiating, making deals, getting information, making sales, joint ventures, and team building, to name but a few areas.

Central American–American Interaction

Americans are much more task oriented than relationship oriented. The goal of business interactions is to get in there, get down to business, cut a deal, and get out, preferably as quickly as possible. The American legal system facilitates this approach, because one has legal recourse if one party to an agreement does not uphold his responsibilities. Trust is placed in the legal obligations (and penalties) to ensure that transactions occur fairly.

In Central America, trust is placed in the people with whom you are doing business, not in an external legal framework. In order to do business, you must first build a relationship. As mentioned in the section on time, new business partners will establish a rapport by learning about each other's families, about who the other person is.

While a personal relationship may develop along with a business relationship in the United States, it is not very common. Business socializing tends to revolve around common business topics rather than personal lives. It is difficult for many American business people to invest time in building a relationship, which they may well consider too intrusive, when they would rather just immediately tackle the problem, negotiation, or other business at hand. Of course this approach is liable to leave a Central American unwilling to commit fully until he is more comfortable with the individuals involved.

Rule Abiding Versus Rule Bending

A subset of the relationship-versus-task puzzle is the issue of relationships vis-à-vis rules. Should rules (both actual laws and the unwritten rules of society) have a universal application, or is there room to maneuver—or even circumvent them?

Central Americans are rule benders in the sense that they will look at the particulars of each situation rather than applying a universal rule to all cases. In almost every case, loyalty to a family member or friend is grounds for bending the rules. Someone who is in a position to "facilitate" the awarding of a contract will do so for a friend, even if the friend wasn't the lowest bidder. This bending of the rules can range from small favors from a personal contact to an outright bribe (*mordida*) when one doesn't have the necessary contacts.

This can be disconcerting to Americans, who prefer a more egalitarian application of rules. Using personal contacts smacks of favoritism or nepotism, which are not looked upon favorably. By the same token, Central Americans can find the American approach cold—why have friends if you can't help each other out when possible? While each approach works well in its respective context, it isn't surprising that they encounter difficulty when they cross the border. A Mexican who attempts to bribe an American policeman when he is stopped for speeding is more likely to have an added fine than an overlooked violation, while an American in Mexico may find it difficult to compete when they "play by the rules."

Tips on Building Relationships

- Take the time to build relationships. It cannot be emphasized enough that relationships are the key to success in Central America. Very little is accomplished in the absence of a personal relationship.
- Be prepared to invest in the relationship over the long term, not in terms of money, but in terms of your time, both professional and personal.
- A business relationship is likely to extend outside of the office walls. Whenever possible, accept invitations to lunch, dinner, or drinks, and view them as an opportunity to build the foundations of your friendships. And don't forget to reciprocate!

REASONING

As Guillermo Herrera made his presentation on the new compensation plan for the company's managers, he became increasingly aware that the Americans in the office were fidgeting, shifting in their seats, glancing at their watches, and looking forward through his handouts, virtually ignoring what he was saying. While he wondered at the rudeness of their behavior, he also worried that they weren't happy with what they were hearing. He wasn't sure why—he had spent a great deal of time compiling all of the information they would need, from the origins of the idea for the new plan to the details of how the decisions were made. He was appalled and embarrassed when some- one eventually interrupted to remind him that they were close to the end of the meeting and asked him to just skip to the implementation strategy for the plan.

Pragmatic, Analytic, or Holistic Reasoning

Perhaps the most complex manifestation of culture is found in our thought processes. Around the world, the ways people reason can be divided into three general styles: pragmatic, analytical, or holistic.

Pragmatic thinkers begin with the goal and seek the steps that will enable them to attain that goal. The emphasis is therefore on finding practical ways to solve a problem or reach an objective. For example, if the goal is to increase sales by 10% in a given year, the task is then to identify the means of doing so. A pragmatic thinker will, for example, compile information on increasing his or her client base and the purchases made by current clients. The pragmatic thinker's final report might include a brief mention of all of the ideas presented, but its most prominent point will be the recommendation of certain sales strategies and how best to implement these strategies.

Analytical thinkers take the reverse approach, focusing on the process with the goal as the logical conclusion. So an analytical thinker's approach to the problem above of increasing sales by 10% will be different. He or she will begin by exploring all options, including increasing client base and increasing purchases. From there the analytical thinker will select the strategies that will be the most beneficial, leading to the conclusion that it is possible to increase sales by 10% in a given year. This increase then becomes the goal.

Holistic thinkers incorporate both of the methods above, but they also tend to include elements in their thinking that most pragmatic and analytical thinkers would not. In determining sales, a holistic thinker would examine the information gathered on the potential and current client base, but he or she might also add a few things to the mix. For example, a holistic thinker may ask, what are the possibilities of expanding the current range of products? Even if the pragmatic and analytical thinkers above had thought of this scenario, it is much more likely to be in a linear fashion. That is, a seller of office products who is not a holistic thinker would not get into selling, say, women's lingerie. Holistic thinkers tend to be more non-linear in their thinking and may see a relationship between office products and women's lingerie that pragmatic and analytical thinkers do not, such as the fact that they have a ready supplier of both. Another question that might be asked by a holistic thinker is how growth will impact the sales staff. Will the higher quotas require them to work more hours in the week or spend more time away from their families? Finally, after putting all of the pieces in the puzzle, the holistic thinker will see that it is possible to increase sales by 10%.

As you can see, each of the three scenarios above ended up in the same place: a 10% increase in sales. However, the road taken in each instance traveled through different terrain, even different countries. This difference in reasoning styles has an unmistakable impact on doing business abroad. Its significance is readily apparent in the process of decision-making, of writing reports and making presentations, and even in communicating.

Method of Persuasion

Closely related to the way we process information is the method of argument that persuades us. Am I swayed more by a matter-of-fact presentation of facts and figures or will an emotional appeal work better? It's easy enough to see that a person who prefers an unemotional discussion of facts will probably not respond well to passionate argument, and vice versa.

Central American American Interaction

Americans are renowned the world over for being pragmatic thinkers, while Central Americans are much more analytical. In school we learn problem solving and deductive skills, respectively. This basic processing difference can lead to serious difficulties as we work together. When we relay information or seek to persuade someone else, we unconsciously use the skills and methods that would work on us. And when our need for information (an overview versus details) or method of argument (fact based versus an emotional appeal) differs, we find we aren't very successful in relaying that information or convincing the other person.

In order to communicate successfully with someone, you must first determine how he thinks; matching your communication style to his processing style is half the battle.

Tips on Reasoning

- Understanding that Central Americans reason differently is the first step, and perhaps the easiest. Much more difficult is modifying your own style to be successful. Practice developing your style of communication and presentation, and thinking through problems from a different perspective.

- Be prepared for emotional appeals when it comes to making a decision. Often a passionate emotional appeal has a stronger appeal than "the facts." Allow room in your thought process for a more holistic approach to decision-making, including empathy in the equation along with the cold, hard facts.

WHAT DOES IT ALL MEAN?

As you have probably already noticed, there is often a correlation between the above categories. None of the six categories exists in a vacuum. If relationships are more important to you, it follows that you will be more willing to spend time (or waste it, from a task-oriented point of view) getting to know people before plunging into the task; relationship-oriented cultures tend to also be flexible time cultures. Similarly, if strong and harmonious relationships are your goal, that will be reflected in the way you communicate; relationship-oriented cultures also tend to be indirect-communication cultures. You see the pattern.

Even though we share a continent, there are some considerable differences between Americans and our neighbors to the south. In many instances, we're on opposite sides of the categories as we've outlined them. The key to understanding our interaction and avoiding minor and major disasters is to remember at all times that your

friends and colleagues in Mexico and Central America are not motivated by the same forces that motivate you. Your behavior, frankly,
can be just as baffling to them as theirs may be to you. So respect is
called for at all times. It only takes a little bit to bridge these gaps.
Your mantra should be: "Mine is just one culture among many, no
better, no worse, just different."

THREE

LIVING ABROAD: Thoughts Before You Go

Most people face an international move with a combination of excitement and apprehension. Moving within the confines of your home country can be difficult enough; moving across borders adds a whole new dimension of cultural differences, which can magnify the stress we all naturally feel in a new environment.

The single most important thing that you can do to ensure a successful sojourn abroad is to have realistic expectations. Unfortunately, it's difficult to gauge how realistic your expectations are before you go. You can, however, help define your perspective by considering the following points.

- **What do you hope to get out of your stay abroad?** If you will be working while you're abroad, your company will have certain expectations about the goals of your job, but it is up to you to set your own goals for personal and professional development. Be specific. Although "broadened horizons" is an admirable goal, "gaining an understanding of the domestic automotive market" is a marketable skill that you will be able to use. If you will not be employed, it is essential that you make plans now for how you will occupy your time in the new country. What skills and interests do you have that you can apply to your advantage? You will have many options, including volunteering, continuing your education, or developing a hobby or skill into a freelance business.

- **If you have a partner and/or children, are you starting out with a sound relationship with your partner and with your children?** Although it may be tempting to regard an international assignment as a time to make a fresh start, it is not advisable to use the assignment to try to mend a troubled relationship. An inherent problem with living abroad is the stress caused by being in a new environment and the additional stress of confronting a foreign language and culture. A marriage or partnership that is in trouble, or a family with strained relationships, is more likely to crumble with the added pressure. Couples and families who start out with healthy relationships often find that their ties are strengthened by an international assignment. Each person is able to offer the support and encouragement necessary to create a positive environment with open lines of communication.

- **How much do you know about daily life in the country you are moving to?** It's one thing to know about the history of a country, to be familiar with the cultural icons and know where the best hotels are. But how much do you know about the infrastructure of the country? How much does it cost to live there? What is it like to go shopping? What is the definition of "service" in that country? Will you be able to find babysitters, go to a nightclub alone, wear shorts, ski? In other words, will you be able to find all of the things that you count on to make your life easier and more pleasurable? And if you can't, can you live without them or find acceptable substitutes? These are very important questions to answer before you go. Most of the information is not difficult to find if you are willing to look for it. You can use the Internet, find books, or talk to people who have lived there.

Of course, you may not be planning this relocation alone, and, if not, there's a good deal to consider regarding your children and your partner. We'll start with the children.

IMPACT ON CHILDREN

Accepting an international assignment is a decision that affects everyone in your family, including children. Kids react in a variety of ways, with excitement, resentment, and fear. Children can benefit enormously from living internationally. They develop the ability to look at the world multi-dimensionally and to interact successfully with a wide variety of people; they will also tend to be open-minded and less judgmental. Unfortunately, at the beginning of an assignment, those benefits are on a distant horizon. What you have to deal with immediately is getting your children acclimated to their new lives as painlessly as possible.

Any kind of move can be difficult for children; being uprooted from friends and school and getting adjusted to a strange place is not easy. With an international move and the usual questions "Will anyone like me?" and "Will I be able to make friends?," children have to deal with a new culture, where kids may look different, talk differently, or act differently—or all of the above. Fortunately, there are many steps you can take to smooth the transition.

First of all, involve children in the decision to move abroad. That is not to say that you must allow your child the chance to veto the move. The first reaction of most children to any move—domestic or international—is generally negative. (In fact, if a child reacts positively, it may be a sign of an underlying problem. Your child may be viewing the move as an escape hatch.) But you can let your child know as early as possible about the move. Take the time to discuss why the move is necessary. This is especially important for older children and teens. They are old enough to be involved in discussions about why this move will help mom's or dad's career.

Secondly, let your child express all of his or her feelings about the move. A child's emotions will probably run the gamut from anger to excitement at one time or another. Share your own feelings, too. Let your child know that it's a little scary for you, too, but also exciting. Most importantly, let your child know that it's okay to feel anxious, excited, scared, or angry.

Another important way to help children adjust is to talk about expectations. Be optimistic, but prepare to accept the bad as well as the good. Don't hide the fact that it is going to be hard at times, but don't forget to emphasize the positive. Help your kids learn about their destination. Make it a family project in which you all participate. The more realistic your child's expectations are—and your own too, incidentally—the easier the transition will be.

An easy way to ease a transition abroad is to take items from the house and from your child's room that will make the new house or apartment feel like home. Continuity is a key factor in a child's adjustment. Even though it may be tempting to leave a lot of items and replace them when you get to your destination, try to take as many of your children's belongings as possible. It is worth the trouble of packing and shipping if your child's bicycle or her own familiar bed help her to become comfortable with her new home.

Just as you involved your children in the decision to move, involve children in the actual move as much as possible. Children feel helpless during an international move. They are being moved abroad without having much say in the matter. It will help lessen the feeling of helplessness if you let children make as many decisions as you can. Let your child choose favorite toys or furniture, a favorite picture from the living room, or other items that you will take with you.

Allow your children the opportunity to say goodbye to their friends. Have a party and let the children invite their friends, or enlist the help of a teacher in throwing a class party. Take videos or lots of pictures and an album to bring with you. Adults are sometimes surprised that young children have as deep an attachment to their playmates and possessions as older children. With all children, it is important to recognize the sense of loss and grieving that children go through when moving. Making "good good-byes" is an important step in being ready to accept the new.

Finally, make plans for staying in touch with family and friends. Make an address book for younger children to write the addresses of their friends in so that they can write. Think about other ways to stay in touch, such as a round-robin newsletter, faxing, e-mailing, or creating an audio- or videotape that you can send home. Create a schedule for a weekly or monthly telephone call, writing letters, or making your tapes.

There is no formula that you can use to determine how your child is going to react. And obviously two children in the same family can have totally opposite reactions, with one skipping cheerfully off to school right away and one suffering stomachaches that double him over in pain. Personality plays a part in the adjustment, but so do the parents and the environment created in the new home. Following are some descriptions of general behavior patterns. As you read these descriptions, consider how your child has reacted to stressful situations in the past; this will give you insight into how he might react to an international move—which is most assuredly stressful—and give some thought to how you can help him manage his cultural transition.

Infants and Toddlers

While the biggest disruption for infants is the change in sleeping and eating schedules, toddlers will have a harder time understanding what is happening, and will require a great deal of reassurance before, during, and after the move. Distress at this age often results in a regression to babyish, clinging behavior.

Preschoolers

Preschool-age children should be involved in the move as much as possible. Create ways that they can help, such as selecting which toys and clothing to bring and which to leave, labeling the boxes from his or her room, and packing for the trip. Seeing things being put into boxes and knowing that they will be unpacked in a few weeks is reassuring. Games will help explain the move; you can stage a play move with a dollhouse or by packing up and "moving" in your child's wagon. Coloring and activity books and picture books of your destination will add to the sense of security. Don't forget that shipped boxes may take several weeks to arrive. Make sure you take some of your familiar items on the plane with you.

Preteens

Older children will have more questions and will require more explanations. Take the time to discuss why you are moving, and be open about your feelings about moving. It helps children to know that their parents are sad to be leaving behind the people they know but are looking forward to a new experience. Learn with your children about your new country. Make trips to the library and select books that you can read together. Get a world map and a map of the country so they can see where they are going. Work with your children's teachers to make a presentation about the country. Learn about the food, traditional clothing, or holidays of the country. You can also help your children learn some phrases in the new language. Make a game of learning how to say "please" and "thank you" and other simple phrases. And give older children as much responsibility as possible in getting ready to move.

Teens

Teenagers often have the most difficulty with a major move. They are at a time in their lives when they are trying to establish an identity separate from their families and gain independence. The identity being shaped is linked to friends and social activities; changes make things all the more difficult. Moving to another country adds more pressure in the form of a potential language barrier and unknown customs. The best way to help teenagers through this period is through open communication. Let them know that what they are feeling is okay. You can also help by finding out as much information as possible about where you are going. Get information on the new school, including the curriculum and extracurricular activities. Finding out how kids dress and what they like to do when they get together is important, too.

Although living abroad is a rewarding experience, some circumstances make it preferable to allow a teenager to remain behind for the remainder of a semester or a school year (especially in the case of high-school seniors). Include your teenager in the discussion and make the decision based on the needs of your family.

All children, no matter what age, pick up on and, to a certain extent, reflect the behavior of their parents. Therefore, a positive attitude on your part is the best way to influence your children. Your enthusiasm and acceptance of your new life will help them adjust; the way you handle your own frustrations will set the example for them.

IMPACT ON SPOUSES OR PARTNERS

In the majority of cases, expatriates who accompany their spouse or partner abroad are not able to get the necessary permit to work in the host country. If you are giving up or postponing a career or job to make this move with your partner, you are suddenly faced with a great deal of free time that you will have to occupy in the new country.

Giving Up or Postponing a Career

At first glance, having several months—or even several years—of free time may sound like a dream come true. In fact, there are probably few people who wouldn't welcome an extended vacation.

However, you will find that after a couple of weeks of inactivity you will begin to feel restless. For most people, a career provides a lot of their self-identity and feeling of self worth, and its absence will certainly leave a void.

Being a Stay-at-home Parent

When there are children in the family, the accompanying partner often decides to give up his or her career with the expectation that staying at home with the kids will provide more than enough to do. Before making this decision, here are a couple of issues to consider.

- How old are your children?
- Will your children be attending school?
- If your children will be in school, how do you plan to occupy your time when they are gone?
- Are there ways to get involved with your children's activities (i.e., volunteering at the school, coaching, leading field trips, etc.)?

DUELING CAREERS

The most pressing concern for dual-career couples is usually finding a position for the accompanying partner. It is important to stress that while it is not always possible to find a paid position, there are usually plenty of other opportunities. The best way to find a "job" while you are living abroad is to redefine what "work" is. Broaden your definition from a nine-to-five job to include a host of other things, such as volunteering (which may lead to a paid position), freelancing, consulting, continuing your education, or learning new skills.

The following questions will help you begin to plan for identifying an occupation while you are abroad.

- Is it possible to get the permit you need to be eligible to work in that country? Can your company or your partner's company help you obtain one?

- Are there any opportunities within your company in the new location (either in a local office, if there is one, or as a consultant or working on a project for your company that can be accomplished from abroad)?
- Are there any similar opportunities within your partner's company?
- Are there entrepreneurial possibilities that you can pursue while abroad?
- Does either your company or your partner's company offer any type of career counseling or job location assistance that would help you find a suitable position abroad? (This can sometimes be negotiated as part of the relocation package.)
- Are there volunteer opportunities in your field that you would consider appropriate substitutes for a paid position?
- Are there other opportunities outside your field that you would consider appropriate substitutes for a paid position?
- Do you have a hobby or other interest that you could capitalize on? For example, if you have an interest in photography, can you freelance or assist a professional photographer?
- Is this an opportunity to make a career change? You will have a period of time that you can put to use learning new skills or developing your skills in a different direction.

So far in this section we've taken a look at some important points to remember when considering the impact of a move abroad on yourself, your children, and your partner. Another major issue is cultural adaptation, or, in other words, what you should expect as you look ahead at your and your family's acclimation to a new culture.

UNDERSTANDING CULTURAL ADAPTATION

Culture shock, or cultural disorientation, is the result of finding yourself in a culture that is new and unfamiliar. People in the new culture not only speak a different language, they also live by a different set of rules, with different values, attitudes, and behaviors. In some cases, these differences are immediately obvious; in others they are quite subtle. Cultural disorientation results in a range of emotional reactions, from irritation and frustration to anxiety and insecurity to resentment and anger. If the cultural adaptation process is not well managed, it will lead to depression.

No one is immune to culture shock; even frequent travelers and people who have lived abroad before feel its effect. The exception to the rule is the person who experiences mild culture shock in an abbreviated form. For the vast majority of us, though, culture shock has a significant impact. The key to managing the cultural adaptation process is understanding what it is and developing an awareness of how it is affecting you personally. Once you reach this understanding, you will be ready to take steps to manage the stress caused by culture shock.

Culture shock is an emotional cycle with four distinct periods: enchantment, disenchantment, retreat, and adjustment. Although most people experience all four periods, each person's cycle is different; even different members of the same family will go through the ups and downs at different times.

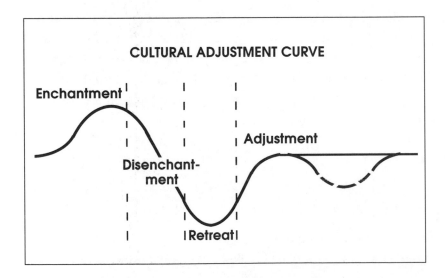

CULTURAL ADJUSTMENT CURVE

Enchantment

Disenchantment

Retreat

Adjustment

Enchantment

Your arrival in your new home is an exciting time. Your senses are operating at top speed as you try to assimilate all of the new sights, sounds, and smells. You want to see and do everything. There are many new things to learn and discoveries to make. The differences that you notice between your home country and your new country are charming.

Disenchantment

After several weeks, a period of disenchantment typically sets in. As you establish your routine in your new country, reality begins to intrude on your enchantment. You have to deal with the mailman, the plumber, and your neighbors. Even simple tasks become difficult. When you go shopping, you may not recognize foods or be able to find what you want and what you're used to. People may seem rude, overly friendly, or just plain different. It is emotionally taxing to speak a new language, to use a new currency, and to perform all of the other minor details that you never gave a second thought to at home. With the new reality comes a sense of frustration and irritation, and often insecurity, since all of the cues you never had to think about before have changed.

Retreat

As you begin to feel more and more frustrated, tension and resentment will begin to build up. The retreat stage of the adjustment cycle is the most difficult. It becomes harder to leave your home. If you work, you may find yourself working late or coming straight home from the office. You turn down invitations and minimize contact with the culture and people in the new country. What was once "charming" or "interesting" about the country and customs has become "strange" and "stupid." In the constant comparison between your home country and the host country, home wins hands down. Homesickness is acute.

Adjustment

Finally, you will have to make the effort to adjust, to reestablish contact with the world and go on with your life. Your attitude will determine how you reconcile yourself to the things that are different in your new country. The people who make the most successful adjustments are those who realize that there are things that you like and dislike in any culture; doubtless there are things that you didn't care for at home, too. If you are willing to accept the culture, enjoy the things that you love about the culture and find ways to accommodate the parts that you do not like, you will be happy. Once you have managed a successful adaptation, you will realize that you have gained a new set of skills, and are able to operate effectively within a new culture.

And Beyond

If you take another look at the Cultural Adjustment Curve, you will notice a second dip. Many people experience a second low period, or even a series of ups and downs. Just when you think you've finally got things figured out, you stumble again. A subsequent period of disillusionment might be more or less severe than the first; either reaction is normal.

KEYS TO A SUCCESSFUL ADJUSTMENT

The keys to a successful adjustment are self-awareness and acceptance. In order to be able to recognize cultural differences and effectively deal with them, you must first be aware of your own cultural values and attitudes.

Acceptance, the second key, means understanding that the culture, customs, and rules in your new country, however far from your home country, are valid. Once you are able to accept them as different rather than better or worse than your own, you will be more comfortable and able to adapt to new ways of doing things.

Understand that the ups and downs of cultural adjustment are normal; everyone who has moved before you has experienced the same process, complete with similar symptoms. If you reach out to those people, they can help you through the process. They will tell you that they survived and so will you.

Even after you have adjusted, you will have good days, when you feel at ease in your new culture, and bad days, when you question your sanity in deciding to move there. Once you have completely adjusted, the good days will eclipse the bad.

Coping Techniques

The psychological disorientation of an international move causes a tremendous amount of stress. In order to manage your cultural adaptation successfully, you must find an outlet for this stress. Think for a moment about how you relieve stress in your life right now. Stress outlets can be physical, such as jogging or biking, or mental, such as meditation or reading. List your stress relievers on a piece of paper. Once you've made your list, think about how you can continue those activities in your new home. Some of them—meditation, for instance—are easily transported. Some, however, may require modification or planning. For example, if you're used to riding your bike through the country lanes near your home but you will be moving to a crowded urban center, you may have to modify your activity. Can you use a stationary bike instead? Are there near-by parks or other areas where you can safely bike?

If you are not sure about the availability of a specific activity, make it a priority to find out. There are many resources, including other expats, people from your new country who may live in your area, consulates, books, and more.

FAMILIES

Families who have relocated to another country move with their own built-in support network to help each member through the process of adaptation. However, relocation also often means that family roles shift. A spouse who was a breadwinner before moving abroad might become a dependent; normally independent children may find themselves dependent on their parents, at least initially.

An international assignment often includes regional responsibilities that require frequent travel or extended business trips. If one partner is required to travel often, the other is left taking on more of the shared responsibilities in order to fill the gap left by the numerous absences. At times one feels like a single parent, even if it's not the case! Of course, the partner who is frequently away can find himself or herself feeling left out of the family upon returning.

All of these changes can be successfully managed if you have open lines of communication. Parents will benefit from talking with each other about the changes that are necessary to accommodate the new situation and by discussing ways that they can support each other to maintain consistency. The whole family will function better if everyone feels comfortable expressing fears and concerns and receives encouragement and support from other family members.

THE NON-WORKING PARTNER

Unlike children and the working partner, a non-working partner faces a new life that is without the inherent structure of school or work. So once the initial settling-in is done, your partner goes to work every day, the children traipse off to school, and you are left with nothing to do. If you were used to working, this is especially difficult. Even if you were not employed prior to the move, you still have left behind all of the familiar routines that filled your day.

According to article after article, many assignment failures are attributed to a non-working partner who is unhappy in the new culture. This puts a lot of pressure on you; but with some effort and planning, you can put that particular worry aside.

In the absence of outside activities, the world of a non-working partner is limited to household chores and the lives of children and the spouse. In the initial months, these same children and spouses have spent the majority of the day coping with their own stresses in the new culture and are rarely in the mood for scintillating conversation when they return to the sanctuary of home.

The more activities that you are involved in, the more fulfilled your own life will be. These activities can include your family, such as volunteering at your child's school, or they can be a pursuit of your own interests. The possibilities are practically endless. Other than volunteering, you can use the spare time to take classes, develop new skills, or pursue a hobby. If you give your imagination free rein, there are plenty of things that you can do. See the dual-career sections throughout the book for other ideas on making the most of your time abroad.

CHILDREN

Children go through their own adjustment process, just as adults do. Younger children often feel frightened in a new location where everything is different from what they are used to: the people may look different, buildings may look different, and things certainly sound and smell different. Sometimes children (and adults, too) become an object of curiosity if they are living in a country where they look greatly different from the locals (for example, a blond child in Japan). They are often uncomfortable being stared at, touched, and patted by curious strangers. Younger children will have difficulty understanding what the move means, and may tend to relate the move to vacations that they have experienced. They may be waiting for the trip to be over and for the family to return to their familiar surroundings at home. When the return home does not happen, they can get very upset. This may not happen for several weeks, or even months, so that a child who seems to have adjusted just fine may have problems down the road. Symptoms of their distress may be quite physical, such as stomachaches, or emotional, such as withdrawal and depression.

Older children who do understand the implication of an international move and who realize that this move is not permanent, may be reluctant to get too deeply involved with friends, trying to protect themselves from the pain of making friends only to leave again after a year or two.

Throughout the process of adjustment, children will experience periods of anger. This is understandable, since they may feel that they have been dragged across the world against their wishes. It is important to allow children, whatever their age, to express their anger and to provide them with appropriate outlets for it.

Keep in mind, too, that younger children may not be able to put their feelings into words. You can help them express their feelings by taking along children's books about moving that will help them find the words to tell you what is wrong.

Naturally, all children will react differently to an international move. The best way to cope is with patience and understanding.

Global Nomads and Third-Culture Kids

Global nomads, also called third-culture kids, are people who have lived overseas before adulthood, usually because of a parent's job. The global nomad is abroad without choice; the parents have chosen an international lifestyle, usually with the expectation that they will eventually return to the passport country. When children live abroad for a long period of time—or even for fairly short periods of time— they become culturally different from the parents. Their whole avenue of cultural exploration is very different from that of one born and reared in one place (as the parents often are).

Living internationally is a unique opportunity for children. It is a heritage that will shape the rest of their lives. While overseas, children develop a whole host of global skills, including multilingual skills, the ability to view situations from two different sides, and mediating and cross cultural skills—simply by living. It is a heritage that can be applied very usefully in today's global arena.

One of the biggest challenges of moving abroad is to maintain the cultural identity of children. Children are absorbing the new culture through school, caregivers, and what they observe in the world around them. "Home" becomes a place to go on vacation once or twice a year. Parents can keep children connected to their own culture in a variety of ways, such as observing the holidays and traditions of their home culture. It is also helpful to keep in contact with what's going on at home, both with friends and family members and through magazines and newspapers.

PARENTING ABROAD

Raising a child abroad is an added challenge. Depending on where you are living, the values may be different than those you want to instill in your children. Children learn not only from their parents, but from school, peers, other caregivers, and society in general. Imagine that you have told your teenagers that they must be a certain age before they can drink, but they are suddenly confronted with vending machines in Japan that sell whiskey with no restrictions. This doesn't mean that Japan has a rampant problem with teenage alcoholism; it simply indicates that Japanese children are governed by different societal and parental restraints than your child is. These kinds of problems are best dealt with by establishing very clear family rules. Have family meetings to establish and reinforce the rules.

A lack of organized activities for teenagers is often a problem. You and your child may have to search actively for the activities he or she likes to do. If you can't find appropriate activities, think about organizing a baseball team, a drama group, or other activities yourself. Encourage your children to bring their friends over, and try to meet their friends' parents, just as you would at home.

In some countries, the expatriate life itself can pose hazards by making children accustomed to a higher standard of living than most people. Some people find themselves in a position to obtain household help. If you have never had this experience, it will take some time to be comfortable having someone work for you. You may have to train the people you hire, and you should definitely be clear on your expectations; do not assume, for example, that your idea of disciplining your children is shared by the person you hire to babysit your child.

If you are lucky enough to have household help, you may find that your children come to expect that someone will pick up after them and believe that they are not personally responsible for any chores. You may want to continue to assign some household tasks to children to reinforce your own values to them.

DUAL-CAREER COUPLES

Dual-career couples with children face the same issues as other families, but with an additional concern: child care. You are leaving behind your own child-care network and will have to rebuild it from scratch. This can be complicated in countries where the extended family plays a major role in child care and public or private care is rare. Even if your children are in school, there may not be structured activities for them to participate in during the time between school and the end of the work day. There are options if you search for them. Think about the following ideas:

- hire an au pair, nanny, or other live-in help
- look for formal or informal networks within the expat community; often there is a system of sharing child care
- if your job has the flexibility, work from home or part time
- approach a neighbor or another family about looking after your child during the day
- find an older person who would be interested in caring for your child (this has the added benefit of providing your child with a "grandparent")

If you are not able to find viable child-care options, you may be able to create something that will meet your needs. And there are sure to be other families who would welcome the alternative. Don't rule out starting a day-care center for younger children or organizing after-school activities for older children.

The most important thing, of course, is that you feel comfortable with your child-care arrangements and that you trust the person who will be caring for your children.

THE SINGLE LIFE

Living abroad as a single person has both ups and downs. Moving to a place where you have no network of friends is difficult; coping with a new country and culture where you may not know how to go about meeting people to create your new social network is even tougher. In many countries, a person's work and home lives are kept quite separate. Social bonds have been formed throughout the years in school and elsewhere; business relationships do not necessarily translate into social relationships. And, in many cases, the family and extended family play a significant role in a person's life, and a great deal of time is spent in family activities. All of this can make it seem impossible for a newly arrived person to meet people and form friendships.

On the other hand, expatriates are often not subject to the same "rules" as everyone else. Most expatriates find people in their host country to be very sympathetic to their situation, interested in learning more about them, and open to the possibilities of a relationship that extends beyond office hours. With luck, you will find yourself the recipient of invitations from your colleagues.

In the final analysis, though, it is up to you to build your new life. There are many avenues open to you. The best way to meet people, in fact, is to simply do something that you like to do. If you like to hike, go hiking; if you like to work out, join a gym. By doing something that interests you, you are putting yourself into situations where you can meet people with the same interests.

Another possibility to explore is the expatriate community. Where there are significant numbers of expatriates, there are usually networks in place, both for business and social purposes. Often there is a newcomer's club that provides activities and events for socializing. In these organizations, too, you will find people who have gone through the relocation and adaptation process and who have first-hand knowledge of what you are experiencing. These can be invaluable contacts throughout your own process of adaptation, giving you the support and encouragement you need or even a shoulder to cry on when necessary.

Singles often have a unique experience abroad. Because they are not accompanied by a family, they generally have much more contact with the language and culture of the host country. An expat with a family goes home at the end of the day, speaks his or her native tongue at home, and is shielded from the language and culture to some extent. A single person does not have that shield, and spends more time speaking the new language and immersed in the culture through his or her social life. That person often has the added benefit of learning the language more quickly and thoroughly and of adapting to the new culture quickly.

THE GENDER FACTOR

The myth that women are not able to be successful in some cultures has largely been debunked. Instead, many experts say that, in fact, women are often better equipped to be successful than men. Most women find that they are viewed first and foremost as foreigners and are therefore not subject to all of the rules that apply to the local women. So even in cultures where women are not traditionally found in business, the same barriers do not apply to foreign women. In fact, many women have found that they can use the curiosity of local businessmen to their advantage and get their foot in the door more easily than their male counterparts.

One issue that women do face, on a very personal level, is whether or not they can accept the local culture—specifically the role and treatment of women. This does not mean that you have to behave exactly like the local women (although there may be certain amount of conformity required of you), but you do have to be able to live with what is happening around you. This is a very personal decision; if you are uncomfortable with a culture's general attitude toward women, then perhaps it is better to wait for another assignment in a country where you feel more comfortable. Take care, though, that you understand the values that underlie the explicit behavior; it is easy to confuse the desire to protect with the desire to restrict.

THE RACE FACTOR

Most people of color find that they are seen first as being American, or Canadian, or British, etc. In countries where there is a history of discrimination against a certain minority group, usually an immigrant group, those rules simply do not apply to expatriates. There is no general formula for the experience that people of color have internationally. As in the case of one African American, some expatriates feel that they actually have an advantage because they are used to being in the minority, which can make the adjustment to the new culture easier than for someone who is used to being part of the majority. As with the gender issue, it is not a question of the situation being good or bad; the issue is how you personally handle being in the limelight. In another case, a woman of Puerto Rican descent who grew up in New York considered herself to be an American and not a minority, with little thought of her cultural roots. When she was given an assignment in Latin America, she began to explore the Latino culture and began to value that part of her heritage.

There are cases, however, where Americans of a particular minority group do encounter difficulty abroad. This occurs most often when a person relocates to his or her ancestral home. For example, a Japanese American might be selected for an international assignment in Japan. Usually the selection is made because of the "Japanese" part of the equation, with little thought to the "American" part. In other words, the selection is made because someone looks the part. This strategy can backfire, though. Even if that person speaks Japanese, he has absorbed the American culture and holds many American values, since that is where he spent his formative years. The difficulty arises because he looks Japanese but does not act Japanese. The result can be suspicion, distrust, or ostracism on the part of the Japanese. Similar situations confront many Asian Americans whose families immigrated generations ago, including "overseas Chinese" and Vietnamese Americans. These issues can be minimized or avoided if you have an awareness of who you are and an understanding of the culture that you will be living in, especially the ways in which it is different from your own blended culture.

SEXUAL ORIENTATION

If you are lesbian or gay, you will probably want to do some research on the acceptance of homosexuals in the country you will be living in before you embark on your international assignment. While some countries have laws preventing discrimination against anyone because of sexual orientation, the acceptance of homosexuals by the society in general ranges from tolerance to homophobia much as it does in the United States. Make sure you are also aware of any laws prohibiting homosexual acts, and the possible consequences of practicing your sexuality. These concerns will affect bisexuals and transgendered people as well.

Moving abroad with a same-sex partner presents certain challenges not faced by married partners, as it is virtually impossible for an accompanying partner to get a work visa without being legally married. In addition, few companies include same-sex partners in the expatriate benefit package, causing complications in matters such as housing allowances, insurance, and allowances for the loss of the partner's income. As an accompanying partner, you must focus on the alternatives that are available to you in the new country. Issues of giving up or postponing a career must be dealt with, and work alternatives must be investigated. Be proactive in exploring your options. Try to talk to people who have experience living in the country, both natives of the country and expatriates who have lived there. The more people you can talk to, the more complete a picture you will have about the implications of being lesbian, gay, bisexual or transgendered in your new culture.

A WORD ABOUT EXPATRIATE CLUBS

Many expats are wary of expatriate clubs, seeing them as a group of spouses who get together to play tennis and bridge. Even if there are people in the organization who do play bridge, the clubs are much more than that. Expat organizations are excellent source of information on everyday issues such as finding a doctor; for networking, something accompanying partners seeking jobs or alternatives can tap into; for learning about the culture through structured activities and events; and for socializing. Each individual can decide how much he or she wants to be involved in the expatriate community. Indeed, there are plenty of expats who immerse themselves in it, and have very little contact with local-country nationals. There are also people who avoid it altogether. You are free to choose either, or any point on the spectrum between. Just keep in mind that the expatriate network can be invaluable; it can also provide that touch of home when you need it.

STAYING IN TOUCH

Even if you are excited about the prospect of living abroad, don't forget to make plans to stay in touch. You will want to hear from your family and friends at home and keep them up-to-date on your own adventures. It's very easy to get swept up in your new life, and difficult to find the time to write or call with all of the new challenges of living abroad. However, the people who form your network of support will continue to be important as you adjust to your life abroad, especially during difficult times.

Establishing and maintaining a systematic way of communicating with home is also critical when it comes time to return after your sojourn abroad—something that is difficult to think about when you haven't even left yet!

ROUND-TRIP TICKET: THE RETURN HOME

Contrary to what you might think, the return home, or repatriation, after an international assignment is often a more difficult transition than moving abroad.

Professional Repatriation

One of the hazards of living and working internationally is that when you return, you can find yourself out of touch with your home office and with changes in your field or profession. Without proper preparation, you may find yourself without an office, without direction, and, indeed, without a job. Many former expats have returned to the home country after a successful assignment, only to have to wait for a suitable position to open up. In addition, many returned expatriates find that their experience abroad, and newly acquired skills and knowledge, are not put to use by the organization. A marketing manager fresh from an assignment in Central America may find herself in a domestic marketing position, with little or no involvement in any Central American markets. Even if the goal of the assignment was your professional development with an eye toward "globalization" or developing the international market, it is difficult to put those lofty goals to work practically. It is up to you to ensure that you are receiving the support you need during the assignment and to plan your strategy for reintegration into the home or local office.

If you moved abroad with your partner but were unable to work abroad, you face some of the same challenges when you return. You may feel that technology has passed you by, or that the skills you used before you moved are rusty from disuse. The best way to counteract this is to think about coming home while you are abroad and make sure that you keep your skills up to date—and maybe even develop new skills or expertise!

Following these steps can ease your professional reentry:

- Set a strategy before you go. Getting the support of upper management is crucial. Make sure you have a clear understanding of the objective of sending you abroad, what your goals are during the assignment, and exactly how you will fit back into the organization when you return.

- Stay in touch while you are abroad. In the case of international assignees, "out of sight, out of mind" holds true more often than not. Remind the home office of all of the points outlined above. Keep them informed about what you are doing and your accomplishments. And keep yourself informed about what is going on at the home office, promotions and staff changes, important policy changes, etc. E-mail and faxes are readily available in most companies; take advantage of technology to maintain contact.

- Find a mentor. In fact, find two or three. Mentors will help keep you in the minds of the decision and policy makers and keep you informed about what's going on at home. Mentoring relationships do not have to be formalized. And by finding several mentors, you won't find yourself returning from your assignment only to find that your champion in the company no longer works there!

- Visit the home office whenever you can. While you are on home leave or a business trip back, take the opportunity to reconnect with colleagues. Make use of the time to familiarize yourself with recent changes. Even if you take all of the recommended steps to stay in touch, understand that things will be different when you return. The fact is, the company and your colleagues have grown in the time you have been away, just as you have. It will take time and patience to reintegrate yourself into the new environment.

Personal Repatriation

Personal repatriation can also be painful. During your sojourn, you will have gained new insights and new perspectives. You will realize that there is really no right or wrong way to do things, only different ways. In addition, most people remember "home" with fondness while they are away, forgetting about the things that aren't so great. And, of course, you will come home to find that your home country has its share of blemishes, just like everywhere else. This means that you will go through another cycle of adjustment as you refamiliarize yourself with your home culture and come to terms with the bad as well as the good in it.

If you are gone for several years, you will experience some disorientation when you return. Things will have changed, and you will have had a long period of time in which you have not shared experiences with your family and friends. You may find that some people aren't interested in hearing about your experiences abroad, or roll their eyes when you say "When I was in...." You may even encounter people who feel that you are putting on airs or that you feel superior because of your experience. You will have to come to terms with the fact that the people you knew before you left have changed, as you have, but in different ways.

There are ways to ease your personal readjustment.

• Stay in touch while you are gone. This can be difficult as you immerse yourself in your new life. Just as you fade from prominence at home, home fades for you. You will have to make a conscious effort to maintain regular contact, and make sure your kids do. The benefit of doing this is that when you return there is less of a void in your experiences; you have kept people informed of important events in your lives, and vice versa.

• Visit home whenever possible. This is especially important if you have children. As well as helping you keep in contact with friends and family, it helps children maintain their sense of "home" and their cultural identity.

• Realize that your return home will have its ups and downs, just as your adjustment to living abroad did.

Children's Repatriation

The most difficult part of readjustment for children is that they have a gap in their lives where they have missed all of the pieces of popular culture that their friends have experienced, such as music, movies, TV, toys, and the way kids dress. They have to learn the current slang, and how kids talk. Along with this, they are different from their peers. They have developed in ways that kids at home have not, and they have a different frame of reference. More than adults, children who return home after living abroad will find that their peers see them as thinking that they are superior and resent references to "When I was in... ."

Tips for Staying in Touch

Most of us are accustomed to picking up the telephone and calling someone whenever we want. If you are living in another country, though, you may find that this isn't as easy any more because of the time difference, poor phone service, or the prohibitive cost of international calls. Here are some suggestions for alternative ways of staying in touch.

- **The old stand-by: Write letters.** Since the advent of the telephone, most of us are no longer letter-writers. When phoning is too expensive, this is one of the cheapest alternatives. However, it's also the slowest!
- **Fax letters.** Write your letter, then fax it. This will give you the satisfaction of instantaneous communication, without the prohibitive cost of an extended telephone call. Family and friends without a fax machine can probably arrange to receive faxes at a nearby copy shop or similar service center.
- **E-mail.** Probably the least expensive alternative, although not an alternative in all locations.
- **Chatting on-line.** If you and your family and friends all have Internet access, and you are able to access the Internet from

your new country, try scheduling a time to find a quiet on-line corner to chat. Some of the larger services such as CompuServe and AOL offer service in many countries. Just remember that you may have to pay for local connect time rates—check with your service provider.

- **Use the company's phone.** With the company's permission, of course! As part of the expatriate package, some companies will allow you and your family members limited use of office phones to make international calls.

- **Videotapes or cassettes.** Although they will take a while to get there, videotapes and cassettes are more personal than writing letters. It's especially nice if you have children. You can exchange tapes with family members, and your children can exchange them with friends and even their classes at school. Be sure you will have access to the right equipment, since many countries use PAL instead of VHS. A further word of caution: be careful not to run afoul of the local laws. For example, in some countries, a videotape that includes your sister frolicking on the beach in a bikini may be considered pornography locally, even if you don't think it is. Make sure you know all of the applicable laws.

- **Write a newsletter.** This is especially helpful if you've got a long list of people you want to keep in contact with. Document what is happening in your life, write about the funny things that happen, about current events in your new community, or anything else that appeals. Or start a round-robin letter, where everyone who receives the letter adds to the letter and passes it on to the next person.

- **Schedule regular phone calls.** It's bad enough to reach an answering machine when you want to talk to someone. It's worse when you are paying international rates to talk to a machine! If you talk to someone often, try to arrange for a regular time to call—every Sunday night at 10:00, the last Saturday of each month, or whatever fits both of your schedules.

LEARNING ABOUT YOUR NEW HOME

You're on your way to a new adventure. Now is the time to gather all of the information you need to make your international sojourn successful. Learning the language (if it's different from yours) and learning about the culture of your new home should be prioritized.

Learning the language of the country you will be living in is an obvious necessity. If it happens to be a language you already speak, great; if not, get started as soon as possible. Make it your goal to learn at least basic phrases before you go, more if possible. This book comes complete with a special language section and an audio CD for just that. While some people have a facility for learning languages, others find it more difficult. And it is often more difficult for adults than for children. Yes, you will make mistakes, and even embarrass yourself. It will be frustrating to have to struggle to express yourself, and you will feel awkward speaking with a limited vocabulary as you start out, but the effort is well worth it. The fact that you are willing to make the effort to adjust yourself to a new language will open many doors for you, and you will find that most people respond with delight. Learning the language also gives you the opportunity to really experience life in the local community in ways that are not possible if you are isolated from interaction by not speaking the local language.

Just as important as learning the language of your new country is learning about its culture and peoples. What are the values that the people hold, what is their history, what are their beliefs, customs, and traditions? In the Background section of this book, we've provided you with enough of this kind of information to whet your appetite. Don't stop there, though! There are lots of ways to go about learning about the culture of your new country, including reading books and articles, talking to other expats or people from the country, and participating in a pre-departure (or post-arrival!) cultural orientation. Don't expect to learn everything there is to learn about the country in such a short time, or imagine that you will be prepared for every contingency; your goal is to learn enough to be comfortable in your new home. Once you arrive, you will discover on your own much more than you can ever learn from a book or from talking to other people.

Perhaps the first step in learning about your new culture is to learn about yourself and your own culture. Because culture is such an innate part of who we are, few people take the time to ponder what it is that makes them tick. Spend some time reflecting on your own cultural heritage, and ask yourself the same questions you would ask of another culture: What are your values, what is your history, what are your beliefs, customs, and traditions? The more you understand about yourself, the easier it will be for you to recognize cultural differences and reduce the likelihood of cultural misunderstandings.

MOVING ABROAD "DOS & DON'TS"

DO...
...have realistic expectations
...find out as much as you can before you go
...learn the language—at least basic phrases
...be open-minded
...find several mentors and cultural guides
...make plans now for keeping in touch
...take the initiative and reach out

DON'T...
...lose touch with family and friends
...wait until it is time to return to plan
     for your repatriation
...wait for other people to come to you

FOUR

GETTING AROUND IN MEXICO AND CENTRAL AMERICA

SAFETY

Like any other place in the world, Central America has its share of crime. Throughout Central America's cities there are areas that are more dangerous than others, which should obviously be avoided. If you are unfamiliar with the territory, you can ask a friend or colleague, the staff of the hotel where you are staying, or even a taxi driver to alert you to those places that are best avoided.

Pickpocketing, purse snatching, and even hold-ups do happen. The same rules that apply when traveling or visiting new places in your own country apply. For example, don't flash expensive jewelry or camera equipment. Keep your cash in a safe place. Be alert and aware of strangers. Don't allow yourself to be distracted, leaving yourself vulnerable to a pickpocket. Stay out of dangerous areas and be careful how and where you get around after dark. And so on. Just using your common sense can keep you out of most trouble.

Be aware, too, that political instability in some areas makes traveling potentially more dangerous. Foreigners can be targeted or may just be in the wrong place at the wrong time. The best advice when traveling through Central America is to keep up with current events in the places where you will be traveling and avoid the hot spots. The U.S. State Department or your local embassy or consulate can be a good source of information regarding travel. The U.S. State Department routinely issues travel warnings and advisories on international travel; check their website at www.state.gov.

TOILETS

Toilets can be tricky business when you are traveling abroad. In Central America you will find the kind that you are used to—the sit-down kind. However, most public places do not have a water supply sufficient to handle waste paper. Therefore, you should discard your toilet paper in the waste receptacle next to the toilet unless there is a sign specifically stating that you can flush it. It is very important that you observe this rule so that the sewage system does not get blocked.

Public rest rooms are available in many places; many charge a few cents for their use. However, toilet paper is not universally available in public, hotel, or restaurant bathrooms. Some public rest rooms have an attendant who gives you a few squares for a small tip. The best advice is to make sure to always carry some tissues around with you in case you need them.

DRIVING IN CENTRAL AMERICA

While you can get by with a valid foreign driver's license in many countries, it is advisable to obtain either an International Driving Permit or an Inter-American Driving Permit. The latter is essentially a Spanish translation of your foreign driver's license. Having one of these can help avoid potential problems that could arise if you should encounter a police officer who is unable to read your driver's license. Both documents are available from the American Automobile Association or Canadian Automobile Association.

Road conditions vary throughout Central America. In general, highways and major roads are reasonably well maintained. Secondary roads, however, can range from good to adequate to barely passable. If you are unaccustomed to mountain driving, travel on the steep grades and sharp curves in the highlands will take some getting used to. Driving on unpaved roads during the dry season is dusty but usually without problems. The dusty road you navigated easily during a dry month will turn to mud during the rainy season, making travel much more difficult. Therefore it can be a good idea to ask a local, perhaps at a nearby gas station, about the condition of secondary roads before you venture onto them. If you will be doing a lot of traveling by car, it's advisable to have a sturdy vehicle with a high clearance, such as a jeep or pickup truck. This applies to rental vehicles as well, since you may be responsible for damage to the car, and driving in Central American can take a heavy toll.

When you're driving outside the larger cities, don't take gas stations for granted, especially off the major roads, where they are few and far between. In remote areas it's a good idea to carry extra gasoline and water with you. And remember that gas prices are high throughout Central America.

In many places it is customary to beep your horn when approaching a curve on narrow roads to warn any vehicle that might be coming the other way. On roads where there is no shoulder, a branch placed in the road may be a warning that there is a disabled vehicle ahead; you should follow this practice if your vehicle breaks down. If you need directions, good luck! A lot of people throughout Central America tend to navigate by landmarks rather than by addresses or mileage. The problem is that they also have a habit of referring to structures that are no longer there, which is less than helpful to someone who hasn't lived there long. It's always a good idea to confirm that the landmarks mentioned are still in existence, or get clarification when someone directs you to turn left "after where the bus station used to be."

It isn't uncommon for police officers to be offered or to expect a bribe when they stop vehicles for traffic violations or speeding. If the police officer who stops you seems to be taking an excessive amount of time, he may be waiting for a bribe. However, be aware that offering a bribe can be risky business for a foreigner. Instead, you can explain that you are not familiar with all of the local driving rules, which may result in more lenient treatment. Be sure to remain respectful throughout any encounter with law enforcers.

Of course, while you are traveling throughout Central America, you will need to use your common sense. For example, leaving things in plain view in your car is inviting a break-in, so you will need to put everything in the trunk before leaving your car. If you are traveling in an unfamiliar area, you can always ask someone—a friend or colleague, the hotel concierge, or the taxi driver—if there are areas that are dangerous and should be avoided.

Driving conditions vary throughout Central America, although the rules of the road will not be significantly different from those of most Western countries. Remember, though, that is your responsibility to familiarize yourself with the driving rules and laws in each country; ignorance is not an excuse if you get stopped.

Some of the common denominators you might encounter are:

- Many people have a bad habit of driving at night without their headlights. If possible, avoid driving at night.
- As we've already mentioned, a tree branch placed in the road may indicate a stalled vehicle ahead; approach with caution.
- A quick tap on the horn is common when approaching a curve on a narrow road or one with no shoulder, or when passing another vehicle.
- Arm gestures are commonly used to ask that you let the other driver cut in front of you.
- There are many steep, narrow roads. Yield the right of way to the vehicle coming uphill.
- It is not uncommon to encounter pedestrians and animals on the road; always be alert.
- Many countries have routine police checkpoints, and you must be able to produce your driver's license and the papers for the vehicle.

If you are planning a trip through several countries, you should be aware that many car-rental companies do not allow renters to drive their cars across certain borders. Check with the rental agency before you drive off the lot. Rental companies in some areas are also notorious for charging multiple times for any damage to rentals, so be sure you thoroughly check the car over and have the attendant note any preexisting dents and dings. Car-rental insurance may be expensive, inadequate, or unavailable, and the deductibles are generally very high. If you wish to have insurance, the larger international companies tend to have it more readily available. You may also want to check with your own insurance agent to see if your policy extends to rental cars, or even your credit-card company, since many gold and platinum cards offer some protection for rental car damage.

FOCUS: MEXICO

DRIVING

Driving in Mexico City can be quite trying, as traffic congestion abounds. Most Mexican drivers consider the posted speed limits to be merely a suggestion. Take care to stay with the flow of traffic; driving too slowly can be even more dangerous than driving too fast. If you need help while you're on the road, keep an eye out for the *Angeles Verdes*, or Green Angels, who patrol tourist routes between 8:00 A.M. and 8:00 P.M. (except Tuesday mornings) to aid motorists who have run into trouble. They can often make minor repairs on the spot. The *Angeles Verdes* travel in green pickup trucks that have "Tourist Assistance" written on the side.

If you park your car in a no parking zone, you may return to find that your license plate has been removed by the police. You must go to the local police station to retrieve it after paying the applicable fine.

PUBLIC TRANSPORTATION

Subways

Mexico City has an extensive subway system that offers modern, convenient transportation throughout the city. The system, commonly called the Metro, operates from 6:00 A.M. to 12:30 A.M. One ticket will allow you as many transfers as necessary to reach your destination. Tickets are available at booths at the subway stations and can be purchased in multiples. As is the case with most public transportation, the rush hour means crowded trains.

Buses

An extensive network of city buses is available in all urban areas, although the quality of service and facilities varies from location to

location. In large cities the buses can be crowded and uncomfortable. The route may be long, depending on traffic congestion. Shuttle buses that operate in many downtown areas offer an alternative to city buses.

Intercity buses are available for travel throughout Mexico. There are three different types of buses:

- Local buses stop frequently and travel routes off of the *autopistas* (major highways). These buses tend to be older and less comfortable.
- Regular-service buses travel between major cities with scheduled stops in other medium-sized cities. The buses are more comfortable, but are not equipped with bathrooms, so they stop frequently at roadside cafes.
- Luxury buses are modern, clean, and the most comfortable.

Trains

Mexico's train system, the *Ferrocarriles de México*, is government run, although it is now being privatized. Sleeper cars are available on some major routes for overnight travel. Trains offer first- and second-class service. Second class can be overcrowded.

Taxis

Taxis are readily available in major cities. Most taxis say *Taximetro*, indicating that the taxi is metered. You will want to ensure that the driver starts the meter when you get in to avoid potential fare disputes. Although taxis can be hailed on the street, it is safer to make arrangements through a dispatcher. Do not get into a taxi that you have not hailed yourself. A taxi that pulls up to you to offer its services should be viewed with suspicion.

Especially in larger cities, you will find it easier if you are able to provide the taxi driver with at least the *colonia* (neighborhood) of your destination in addition to the address. Major landmarks in the area can also be helpful.

FOCUS: BELIZE

DRIVING

Car rentals are available only in Belize City. Road conditions are poor throughout most of the country; many roads are unpaved. Unpaved roads alternate between muddy during the rainy season and dusty during the dry season. Choose a vehicle suited to those conditions. There are no traffic lights in Belize, so use caution when driving. Posted speed limits are regarded as merely suggestions by most drivers. Don't try to bribe Belizean police officers.

PUBLIC TRANSPORTATION

Belize has no trains or subways. For getting from city to city within Belize, you can take a bus. However, air travel is probably the most convenient and comfortable way to travel.

Intercity buses are generally crowded and uncomfortable. You can buy a ticket ahead of time to ensure a seat. You can also pay the driver, but you will have to take your chances on finding a seat. You'll have better luck finding taxis in Belize City than in smaller towns. They can be hailed on the street, if you can find one, or you can call for one. It's best to avoid people who approach you offering their services as a guide. If you are interested in a tour, you can contact the Belize Tourist Office or ask at a reputable hotel.

FOCUS: COSTA RICA

DRIVING

Costa Ricans have a unique approach to directions. Street names and numbers are of little use. Instead, directions use landmarks and the distance your destination is from them. Don't be surprised if you are given directions that include landmarks that no longer exist—a real test of ingenuity for newcomers!

Rental cars are widely available in larger cities. But keep in mind that defensive driving is a must throughout Costa Rica.

PUBLIC TRANSPORTATION

City buses are run by individual companies with varying fares. The condition of buses varies. Most are not air-conditioned. More modern buses are more expensive. Pay your bus fare to the driver; you do not need exact change. For intercity bus travel, you can purchase a ticket in advance at the bus terminal or simply pay the driver.

Taxis are an inexpensive alternative to bus travel in cities. Most are clean and well maintained. While taxis have meters, it's a good idea to know about how much the trip should cost.

There are a handful of trains between major cities. Service is slow, and the trains make many local stops. Consider traveling by air as an efficient and economical alternative to intercity buses or trains.

FOCUS: EL SALVADOR

DRIVING

If you need to rent a car, you will be able to do so in San Salvador. Major international rental companies, as well as some local companies, have offices at the airport and downtown. Rental rates are relatively high. When you rent a car, be sure that it is appropriate for the terrain you will be traveling on, especially if you will be driving outside the city.

If you're driving your own car into El Salvador, you will be required to show your driver's license and proof that you own the car. Car insurance is not required, but always a good idea.

Carjackings do occur, as does the theft of car parts. Avoid the worst areas and park in a safe neighborhood or in a guarded lot to help reduce this risk.

When you're driving, stay alert at all times. Don't be surprised if you have to brake for cows, chickens, or children in the road, or a car driving on the wrong side of the road. It's common to tap your horn lightly before making a sharp curve on a narrow road or when passing. Hand signals are frequently used to indicate that the driver wishes to cut in front of you or to wave you in.

Road conditions are generally not good, and potholes pock the roads. The constant downpours during the rainy season take their toll, but it doesn't make sense to make repairs until the season has ended. Roads, especially minor ones, are not well marked. You may encounter police checkpoints, especially near the borders.

PUBLIC TRANSPORTATION

Domestic flights are available on Transportes Aéreos de El Salvador (TAES) from the San Salvador airport, but El Salvador is such a small country that it doesn't really make sense to fly within the country.

For travel within El Salvador, buses run frequently to many cities and towns, and fares are inexpensive. Note, however, that there is a 50% fare increase on weekends. Even with the increase, though, rates are much cheaper than in the United States. For intercity travel you have the choice of *regular, directo,* or *preferencial* service. *Directo* and *preferencial* are more expensive but faster. Don't expect a luxurious ride. Prepare yourself for a bumpy road in rather cramped conditions. Take some precautions when you take the bus to avoid potential problems: sit near the front and befriend the driver, who will most likely watch out for you.

Taxis in El Salvador are bright yellow and can be easily found in San Salvador and other larger towns. If you can't flag one on the street, you can call for one. Fares are inexpensive compared to those in the United States. You will want to negotiate the fare before you get in, so try to have an idea of how much it should cost; ask a colleague or the hotel staff if you are not sure.

FOCUS: GUATEMALA

DRIVING

When you drive, be sure to carry your passport, in case you encounter one of the many army checkpoints on the main roads. Road conditions are pretty good throughout the country. Traffic lights are turned off after 8:00 P.M. Driving after dark can be dangerous due to drunken drivers and cars driving without headlights. If you encounter a military vehicle on the road, keep well back from it.

Rental cars are available in Guatemala City, although prices are higher than in the United States or Canada. Your liability for damage to a rented vehicle is substantially greater in Guatemala, with deductibles up to $2,000. If you purchase insurance locally, it will not cover the entire deductible. Check with your insurance agent to confirm what type of coverage your policy offers for rental cars, or consider using a credit card that offers additional coverage for rental vehicles.

Túmulos! *Bumpy road ahead!*

You decide to venture off the beaten path onto a dry, dusty little road just to see where it goes. You see a handwritten sign that says *pendiente peligrosa*. Just as you are mulling over the possible meaning of the sign—you know that *peligrosa* means dangerous—you crest the rise in the road and see that the road drops at an alarming angle and can only be described as winding. You will definitely have to look up *pendiente peligrosa* in the dictionary!

In Guatemala, most major roads have signs with easily recognizable symbols. Signs on secondary roads, on the other hand, are often hand-painted or just plain nonexistent. These are some of the signs you might see:

túmulos	bumpy road
pendiente peligrosa	dangerous grade
frene con motor	downshift, brake with your motor
derrumbes	landslide zone

PUBLIC TRANSPORTATION

Taxis do not use meters, so you will need to negotiate the fare in advance. Tipping is not necessary unless the driver performs some additional task, such as carrying your luggage.

Guatemala has one train that runs from Guatemala City to Puerto Barrios. If you opt for the train, you're in for a long and arduous trip. The trip can take over 20 hours; the same trip by bus takes about six hours.

Local buses travel in major cities. You can buy your ticket from the driver. Keep your ticket for spot checks by inspectors. If you need to travel between cities, you can choose to travel first or second class. First-class buses are usually used Greyhound buses. Although they have toilets on board, they may or may not work. Second-class buses are akin to used school buses and are usually crowded. Buses make occasional bathroom stops. You can purchase a ticket for a reserved seat in advance at the bus terminal. Just pay the driver on second-class buses; reserved seats are not available. Fares may be doubled during Holy Week (Easter). Good Friday is especially tortuous, as everyone else is traveling home to their families.

Ruleteros travel established routes in cities. The fare is based on the distance you travel. Since you may not be able to distinguish them from a taxi, ask the driver before you get in to make sure you're getting on a *ruletero*.

FOCUS: HONDURAS

DRIVING

Honduras has an extensive network of roads crisscrossing the country. Main roads are usually well maintained, local roads often less so.

Use caution during and just after the rainy season, as the weather can cause heavy wear and tear on roads. Signage is generally poor; stop and ask for directions if you are unsure. Speed limits are often not posted; if they are, they are regarded as merely a suggestion. You can drive in Honduras with your U.S. driver's license or an International Driver's License (available from the AAA). However, if you will be staying in Honduras for an extended period, you can easily apply for a local driver's license.

Rental cars are somewhat more expensive than in the United States. If you rent a car, make sure you understand the rules. You will probably not be allowed to take the car outside the country, and you will have to pay extra if you will be dropping the car in a different city. More cars use leaded gasoline rather than unleaded; find out which one the car you are driving requires. Most gas pumps are calibrated in liters. The price on the pump may be pre-inflation. The real price in that case is essentially double the listed price; the attendant can tell you.

PUBLIC TRANSPORTATION

Public transportation in Honduras is limited. There are a few hundred miles of train tracks in the northern part of the country, but train travel is generally uncomfortable and slow.

There is deluxe bus service between major cities. The buses are modern, comfortable, and clean, and offer amenities such as rest rooms, refreshments, and even movies. Bus fare is quite inexpensive. Other areas off the main routes are served by buses and minivans. Schedules are infrequent, and the vehicles are generally old, uncomfortable, and crowded. There are no designated stops between terminals; travelers flag down the bus from the roadside and passengers call out when they want to disembark. In some areas, a shuttle serves the region using more modern vehicles. This service is less frequent and more expensive.

Consider flying as an alternative to traveling within Honduras. It is inexpensive and safe. But be prepared to be patient when it comes to delays caused by flying conditions and schedule changes.

Taxis are often preferable to driving in cities, since the fares are quite reasonable. Taxis don't use meters; you should agree on the fare before getting in. Ask someone at your hotel or a colleague to tell you how much the fare should be to your destination. If the taxi driver won't agree to a reasonable fare, simply hail another taxi. When you arrive, pay only the amount agreed upon, preferably with exact change. Don't tip unless the driver has performed an additional service, such as carrying your baggage, which would earn him a very modest tip. It is possible to hire a taxi for a full or half day at very reasonable rates, eliminating the need to hail a series of taxis throughout the day. And finally, don't expect the driver to speak English. It can help to have the destination written on a piece of paper to show the driver.

FOCUS: NICARAGUA

DRIVING

Rental cars are available in Managua at the airport or downtown. You can choose to rent from one of the international agencies that have an office there or rent from a local company. Expect rental rates to be high. Roads are generally poor throughout the country. Potholes abound and repairs are intermittent at best, leaving you with a bumpy ride. You will probably encounter police checkpoints along the way if you drive much in Nicaragua. They are usually looking for firearms; simply cooperate and you won't run into trouble.

Road signs are generally adequate in larger towns, but you are largely on your own outside the city. Your best bet for getting directions is a nearby gas station. Asking a passerby might get you a positive response but not necessarily the correct information, since people prefer to be polite and encouraging rather than saying they don't know. Ask about road conditions while you are at it.

PUBLIC TRANSPORTATION

Domestic flights are available on several local airlines. Tickets can be purchased in advance from travel agents or at the airport terminal. Most travelers suggest that you reconfirm the return leg of your flight immediately on arrival at your destination.

Buses serve most cities and towns and have the cheapest rates in Central America. The tradeoff is that buses are generally crowded and uncomfortable and the ride can be excruciating, given the poor road conditions. Buses are scheduled to arrive before or just after dark; there is no nighttime service. Buses stop frequently along the way to pick up and discharge passengers. You can flag down the bus you want from the road along the route, but you will lessen your chances of getting a seat considerably; it's better to get on at the terminal if possible.

Local bus service is inexpensive and frequent, but the routes can be confusing. Be alert for pickpockets on crowded buses; tourists and foreigners are often targeted.

Taxis can be hailed on the streets in Managua and in larger towns, or you can call. Negotiate your fare before getting into the taxi. It's not uncommon for a taxi to pick up an additional passenger who is traveling in the same direction. Taxis can also be hired for the day or an excursion, and can be a reasonable alternative to the cramped buses.

FOCUS: PANAMA

DRIVING

If you will be in Panama for less than 90 days, you will be able to get by with your valid foreign driver's license, an International

Driving Permit, or the Inter-American Driving Permit mentioned previously. However, if you're planning an extended stay, you will need a Panamanian license. You can obtain one as long as you have a valid driver's license, a passport, and the results of a blood test (which can be obtained at a local clinic). You will have to pay a licensing fee and pass a vision and hearing test. Rental cars are available at major airports and in larger cities with a valid driver's license, local or foreign. The high temperatures in Panama mandate an air-conditioned vehicle.

Road conditions vary throughout the country. The streets within Panama City and Colón are usually in pretty good shape; secondary and rural roads are largely unpaved and pitted with potholes. If you will be traveling outside the city, it is advisable to rent or buy a four-wheel drive vehicle that sits well above the ground. Speed limits vary throughout Panama, from 90 kph (55 mph) on major highways to 40 kph (25 mph) or less in villages. Unfortunately, speed limits are not always posted, so it's wise to be conservative.

When you come to an intersection that has no traffic light or stop sign, remember that *avenidas*, which are larger streets, have the right-of-way over *calles*, which are smaller streets. And speaking of *avenidas* and *calles*, traffic jams are a problem in the largest cities. During those times, the local police often turn off the traffic lights and have officers present to direct traffic manually.

If you return to your parked car to find a ticket on the windshield, don't ignore it. You will not be able to renew your vehicle documentation and you may be prevented from leaving the country if you have unpaid tickets of any kind, including parking tickets. You can pay your tickets at a branch of the post office, at the *Municipio*, or at the Ministry of Treasury and Finance in Panama City.

PUBLIC TRANSPORTATION

Taxis are usually easy to find. They are not metered, so you will need to agree on a fare in advance. Note that taxis that are larger cars charge more than smaller ones. While it is not necessary to tip the driver, it's customary to round the fare up to the nearest dollar or half dollar. Most taxi drivers will speak at least some English.

Buses in Panama run on irregular schedules and are usually crowded and can be dangerous. It's generally advisable to travel locally by taxi and between cities by plane rather than taking the bus; both taxi and air fares are quite reasonable. *Chivas* are buses that travel regular routes through the cities. Let the driver know when you are ready to disembark; pay when you exit.

While there is a train that travels between Panama City and Colón, the track is poorly maintained, the seats are largely uncomfortable, and the schedule is limited.

FIVE

LIVING IN MEXICO AND CENTRAL AMERICA

Whether you are moving to a new city or a new country, you probably have a long list of questions about your new home. This section addresses some of the important topics faced by families and individuals moving to Central America. If you are moving to Mexico or Costa Rica, Central America's most popular destinations for expatriates, you will find some additional information specific to those countries following the general overview.

HOUSING

Finding a place to live is probably the most important concern of newcomers to any country. There are a variety of options throughout Mexico, from apartments to spacious homes. There are many factors to consider when selecting your new home, including location, cost, and the terms of the lease agreement or purchase.

Location can be the most important determinant for selecting a new home, especially for families that have children. Parents often prefer to first select the school that their children will be attending and from there choose a home that is convenient to the school.

There are neighborhoods in most major cities that cater largely to expatriates. However, you certainly aren't limited to these areas. Many expatriates have found that their experience abroad was greatly enriched by their decision to live outside the expatriate communities, where they could interact with their Central American neighbors in all aspects of their lives.

Things to Think About

- Most housing in Central America does not have central heating or air conditioning. Indeed, they're not needed in many places. Find out what the local weather is in the hottest and coldest times of the year to determine what kind of climate controls you will need. Be sure to add that question to your list when you are looking for a place to live.

- Thinking about taking the washer with you? Because the water pressure is limited in many places, it's a good idea to have a washer that begins the cycle only when the appropriate water level has been reached. A washer that starts the cycle on a timer will not wash and rinse your clothes properly.

- Most North American appliances operate on the same current as you will find in Central America. However, the cost of taking the appliance with you may outweigh the replacement cost. Check to see if a plug adapter will be necessary (remember, if your plugs will not fit in the sockets, you will need to purchase multiple adapters) in your new home. Then find out what the customs duties would be for the appliance(s). Finally, factor in the availability and price of the product locally. A high-tech piece of equipment such as a computer is probably worth the cost of taking yours with you, but are the hair dryer and electric razor?

Most expatriates choose to rent housing for the duration of their assignment. Townhouses, condominiums, and apartments are all popular rental options.

Before you move in, there are several details you should discuss with your landlord. For example, it is very important to clarify who is responsible for the maintenance of your home. Find out if there are any aspects of the upkeep that will be your responsibility. You will also want to verify that the previous tenants have vacated your new home. It can be very difficult for landlords to remove the current tenants, which could leave you without a place to hang your hat when you arrive. Ask for specific details of what does and does not come with the apartment. Many expatriates have been surprised to find that their new unfurnished apartment consisted of four walls and the kitchen sink. All kitchen appliances and even the light fixtures had to be furnished by the tenant.

You can enlist the aid of a real-estate agent in finding a suitable home. If you are planning on buying a home, be sure you use a reputable broker, as real-estate scams are not uncommon. Word of mouth can also be an effective way to locate a place to live. Spread the word around the office, in the expatriate community, in your child's school, and anywhere else you frequent. One enterprising fellow found an apartment by choosing the neighborhood he wanted to live in, then visiting all of the local shops and restaurants asking about available apartments. By showing up day after day, he made himself a familiar figure and found that people were happy to help him.

DOMESTIC EMPLOYEES

Many middle- and upper-class families throughout Central America employ domestic help. Expatriates moving to Central America often find themselves in the unaccustomed role of employer of a maid, housekeeper, and perhaps a gardener. Your maid or housekeeper may live in or she may come to your home several days a week. She either helps out with or is solely responsible for all manner of household tasks, including cooking and cleaning, grocery shopping, and caring for the children.

Although many people relish the break from household chores, they often report some difficulty in adjusting to the role of employer. The most common hurdles are language and training. You will have to find a way to communicate with your employees, since it is unlikely that they will speak much English. This is especially important since you will probably find that their approach to things is different than yours.

A good example is the way that children are treated. Most American families encourage independence and personal responsibility at an early age. Children are encouraged to do things for themselves and help out with chores, and punishment such as "time outs" are meted out for transgressions. In Central America, adults tend to shelter children more and indulge them to a greater extent. Unfortunate expatriate parents have found that after a couple of years with someone who took care of all of the chores, they returned home with a child who didn't understand why he or she now had to mow the lawn or wash the dishes. In blunt terms, a child who was in essence spoiled rotten by home standards.

As a parent, you will have to decide on the household rules in the new environment and what values it is important to instill in your child. Will your child have to clean his or her room or do other chores? How will discipline be handled and by whom? It is important to think about the issues before you hire someone and to communicate clearly your wishes to your help.

BRINGING YOUR BELONGINGS

Household Goods

What do you take with you when you move abroad? Most people find it impossible to bring all the things that they have accumulated over the years with them. The decision of what to bring and what to leave is a very personal one. Some people view a move abroad as a chance to get rid of all but the most essential things and start with a clean slate. Most people find that it makes the transition easier to have at least a few things around that remind them of home. If your family

has children, you may decide to take as much as possible in order to recreate a familiar homey atmosphere to ease the shock of moving.

If you or your family is partial to a particular food item, go ahead and take some along. Although you will eventually be able to find the things you need locally, it can help ease the shock of moving to find your favorite cereal in the cupboard your first morning there.

There are a few basic questions to ask yourself when deciding what to take:

- What do you need to make you feel at home? Moving abroad is a stressful event. It can help if you are able to come home to familiar surroundings. Perhaps there is a painting you love, or a favorite rocking chair you like to read in.
- Is your furniture suited to the local climate and your new home? Perhaps you will decide that your cherished Louis XIV living room fits nicely in your Mexican hacienda; perhaps not. Would it be damaged by the climate and, more importantly, would it survive an earthquake?
- What is available in the country? Is it really necessary to add your refrigerator to the shipment, or can you purchase one just as easily when you arrive? Consider both the cost of shipping and whether or not you will be able to purchase a replacement.
- How much are you allowed to take into the country? Will you have to pay duties or import taxes on anything? Check with your new country's consulate for details.

Vehicles

When you move to Central America, you will have to decide whether you need a car, and, if you do, whether you want to import your car or purchase one once you arrive. The decision, of course, must be made based on your personal situation; there are a few things to consider. Before making a decision, it will be wise to contact the consulate of the country you are moving to in order to get the most up-to-date information on importing vehicles. Import of cars is strictly regulated in many countries, and heavy duties may apply.

What is the cost of shipping your car compared to purchasing a new car? While you may be able to drive down to Mexico City from California, you may not want to make that trip from Toronto or Boston to San José. Note that if you currently lease your car, your lease may prohibit you from taking it outside of the country.

Is your car appropriate to the conditions where you will be living? For example, the roads in many Central American countries, especially in rural areas, are poorly maintained and at the mercy of the elements. Therefore, a vehicle with heavy-duty suspension and four-wheel drive is preferable.

A final note on getting your things from here to there: Laws and regulations are subject to change without notice. In addition, those laws and regulations are often applied arbitrarily by customs officers. Even though you may have had your list of household goods to be imported okayed by the consulate, a customs agent can throw a monkey wrench into the works at the drop of a hat. The result can be hours, or even days, of frustrating delays. Getting your belongings into a Central American country really is the luck of the draw. Many people have reported that they breezed though with no problem; equal numbers have reported delays at the border. For this reason, you may want to consider hiring a professional freight forwarder or other service to handle the details for you—and handle any potential headaches.

Appliances

Because Central American electricity is 110 volts, American and Canadian appliances will work. Some houses have one or more outlets that are 220 volts for certain appliances, such as the washer. Be sure you find out if your home has any 220-volt outlets, lest you blow out your toaster or microwave inadvertently!

In most cases, the plug configuration is also the same—two flat prongs—although you may find an occasional odd configuration. If you are able to take a look-see trip prior to your actual move, put checking out the plug configuration in your new home on your to-do list.

The supply of electricity is uneven in many places, resulting in power surges or brown-outs. For this reason it is wise to take along surge protectors. For your computer and other sensitive electronics, a device that provides uninterrupted power during a power failure is the best choice. These devices will carry you through a temporary failure or surge or give you time to shut down your equipment safely if necessary.

Pets

Pets can be brought to Central America, although the exact regulations differ from country to country and can change. In general, your pet will need to be immunized, usually within a set interval prior to your arrival. A quarantine may be necessary when your pet arrives. Contact the consulate of the country you are moving to for details on importing your pet; your vet can provide you with the necessary immunizations and paperwork.

If you will be staying somewhere temporarily while you look for a place to live, make sure your pet will be welcome there, too. Many hotels do not allow pets.

BANKING

Even if you are on a short-term assignment to Central America, you will still have to take care of financial business, both at home and locally. If you have decided to keep your home while you are away, or if you have credit cards or other bills that will need to be paid, you must make arrangements to take care of this. While you can write checks from your new home, this if often chancy for several reasons. Given the quality of mail service in most Central American countries, it is quite likely that you will have trouble receiving and paying your bills in a timely fashion. In fact, some companies, especially credit-card companies, refuse to mail bills abroad. Most people prefer to make arrangements with a family member, lawyer, account-ant, or bank to take care of their financial matters in their absence.

You will have to choose from several options to find a solution that meets your needs. Some of the possibilities are:

- Maintain your account in your home country and rely on ATMs and/or credit cards to withdraw cash for living expenses. This may work for you if you are on a short-term assignment to a city with electronic access to your funds. For example, in Mexico City you will find many ATMs; in Belize it won't be so easy.

- Maintain your account at home and open a local account for your living expenses. Many people prefer this option, especially in light of the instability of many Central American currencies. If you are exploring this option, be sure you ask the local bank about the details of wiring funds from abroad. Some banks may not have this capability or may take several weeks to make your funds available. Fees will invariably apply.

- Many expatriates open an account with a major international bank, such as Citibank or Lloyds, that offers special expatriate accounts and services that allow them to take care of their finances both in their home country and in the new country from the same bank.

Even if you choose to keep the bulk of your financial business in your home bank, it's advisable to open a checking account locally to take care of your daily and living expenses.

SOCIALIZING

I'm So...Pregnant?!

You are sure to make faux pas as you make your way through a new language. Just be sure you don't make things worse in your apology!

Many words are similar in Spanish and English. For example, restaurant (*restaurante*) or car (*carro*). However, don't get too confident. There are also false cognates, or words that sound similar but have a different meaning. One of the most common, and appropriately, the most embarrassing, is the Spanish word *embarazada*. It may look like it means embarrassed, but in reality it means pregnant.

Names

Hispanic names can be very confusing for Americans. However, they are an important part of people's identity, so it is important to get them right. People may have one or two first names. If someone has a compound first name (María Elena or José María), be sure to use both names.

Everyone has two family names. The first family name is that of one's father, the second is the family name of one's mother. Both names are used when formality is required (a letter, an invitation, etc.), but you will usually call someone only by the first family name. For example, you would address your letter to Juan Carlos González López, but you would call him Juan Carlos González. Remember to learn both family names; you will need to know them when you make introductions, etc. Although using one's first family name is most common, some people choose to hyphenate their two family names (Sergio García-Salas) or to be known informally by their second last name instead of the first.

When a woman marries, she does not take her husband's name. Isabel Fuentes Ortiz marries Manuel Ramírez Díaz, but she stays Isabel Fuentes Ortiz. If she does choose to add her husband's name to her own, it is used with de, so Isabel becomes Isabel Fuentes de Ramírez. A widow who wishes to use her husband's name as part of her own uses *Vda. de* (for *viuda*, widow): Ana Vázquez Vda. de Reyes. Women are never referred to by their husband's first name.

Nicknames are very common. These can be a diminutive of a name (Juanito from Juan, Carmencita from Carmen, etc.) or refer to a personal characteristic. Bear in mind that nicknames are used affectionately, not out of malice. Many an American has been shocked and discomfited to hear someone called *el gordo* (the fat one), or, worse yet, to be called that themselves.

More Notes on Names

María is common as the second of a male's names: José María, Juan María. José is common as the second of a female's names: María José, Isabel José.

Jesús is a common male name. Although it may sound odd to you, remember that Jesus is called Jesucristo in Spanish, so the name is not so strange in context.

Dating and Beyond

It is inevitable that attitudes and behaviors change over the years. When it comes to relationships between the sexes, however, most Central Americans retain more traditional beliefs and customs. Teenagers may go out for group activities, but dating as a couple is more commonly delayed until the late teens and early twenties. Because many couples wait until the man has firmly established himself in an occupation before marrying, the average age at marriage is somewhat higher than in the United States. In addition, the family can be an influential outside pressure on the relationship, given the closer family bonds that are typical. The custom of asking the father of the intended for her hand in marriage is expected.

When it comes to sex as recreation (for men, at least), however, it seems that the United States has the more puritanical society. Prostitution is legal in many places, and sex workers are required to have weekly health exams. (While that may be of some comfort, remember that last week's clean bill of health does not guarantee that this week's sex partners were free of sexually transmitted diseases.)

Sexual Preference

While homosexuality is as much a part of Central American society as it is elsewhere in the world, the region remains largely in the closet. In most people you will encounter a "live and let live" attitude, but there is also the expectation of conformation to certain norms. Most areas have neither a gay-friendly nor a gay-unfriendly atmosphere, preferring to, in effect, ignore the fact that people have different sexual preferences. Very few cities have a gay scene or offer gay-oriented activities. One notable exception is Tegucigalpa, which is home to Prisma (PO Box 4590, Tegucigalpa, Honduras), a gay and lesbian group that hosts discussion groups and activities. Gays and lesbians can expect to live and travel throughout Central America without incident as long as they are discreet. However, there have unfortunately been instances of harassment and abuse of gays, often by the local police or military personnel.

Socializing Tips and Tidbits

Social conversation is an important part of relationships in Central America, and one that too many Americans tend to dismiss. Small talk with strangers should stay on neutral territory: sports, travels, the beautiful surroundings, etc. However, if you are getting to know someone, as a business associate or socially, you will talk about more personal topics, such as your children and family. Even if you are anxious to "get down to brass tacks," you can ruin everything if you don't first spend time on pleasant conversation. Not just a few moments; warm-up conversations that precede a business discussion can take a long time. Try to be patient and don't rush into business.

Many people in Central America dislike giving bad or disappointing news. Therefore, they are more likely to tell you what you want to hear. This does not stem from dishonesty or anything so sinister, but merely from a desire to make you happy. A good example is when you ask for directions. If the person doesn't know how to get to where you want to go, he or she may give you directions anyway. The solution, of course, is to ask several people along the way to confirm your route.

Hold the ¡Hola!

It is a common courtesy throughout Central America to offer a greeting when you enter a restaurant or small shop. In smaller towns, people often even greet virtually anyone they pass in the street. Most of us are familiar with the Spanish greeting "*Hola.*" However, "*hola,*" or "hi," is too familiar a greeting to use with people you don't know. Instead, use *buenas días* (good day), *buenas tardes* (good afternoon) or *buenas noches* (good evening), and save the *holas* for casual situations with close friends.

Miscellaneous

Some people, especially Native Americans in rural areas, do not like to have their picture taken. Ask before taking anyone's picture. It's best not to try to take pictures of airports, military installations or personnel, or other potentially sensitive subjects.

Bargaining is done only at markets and with vendors; expect to pay full price in stores and shops.

Women going to Central America need to know about *piropos*. A *piropo* is a remark, generally flattering but occasionally bordering on vulgar, men make to passing women. A *piropo* can be a simple comment such as *¡Adiós, linda!* (roughly translated as "Hey there, pretty lady!"), a flowery compliment, or a witty remark. The best response to these verbal testaments of virility is no response; simply ignore them. A defensive response is only likely to net you even more unwanted attention.

BARRIGA LLENA, CORAZÓN CONTENTO, OR FULL STOMACH, HAPPY HEART

El amor entra por la cocina.
Love enters through the kitchen.

Central Americans are very proud of their rich heritage and history. One of the more pleasurable ways that this pride is expressed is in the food. There are many regional differences and local specialties. The person who recognizes the special place that food and drink have in the hearts of all Central Americans will reap the benefits— not only gastronomically, but in the goodwill of his hosts.

Sharing a meal isn't just eating. It's an important part of building and maintaining a relationship. The more relaxed, informal atmosphere allows you to get to know one another and enjoy one another's company as friends. Food—lots of it—is what binds people together. Central Americans are generous hosts and will often invite you to their homes for a meal. Following are some tips for a successful dining experience in Central America.

GENERAL RULES OF THUMB

Always try to accept hospitality. Business and socializing go hand in hand. If you consistently reject your colleague's offers of hospitality, you are in effect rejecting that person. Be sure you reciprocate, too. Just as friendship is a two-way street, so is hosting. If you are entertained by a colleague, be sure not to let too much time elapse before you play the host.

Eat what you are served. Who knows—you may even like it! By offering you a special dish, your host invites you to participate in not only the meal, but in the culture as well. Some Central American food is quite *picante*, or spicy hot, and is not like the Mexican food you find in restaurants in the United States. Take small bites and eat rice or tortilla instead of drinking water. Not only is water notoriously hard on foreigners' digestive systems, it's also not as common as a beverage. The blandness of the rice or tortilla makes a much better fire extinguisher.

Don't make negative comments or joke about the food. Put yourself in the other person's shoes, and think about how it would feel if your guest denigrated the food you presented at your table.

Don't eat and run. Mealtimes are about enjoying not just the food but each other's company as well, so allow plenty of time for the fellowship that accompanies the food.

Spouses are generally not included in business entertaining at the beginning of a relationship. Once a friendship is formed, however, spouses often attend. A business meal will usually begin with general non-business topics. Go with the flow and allow your hosts to turn the discussion to business.

Hard drinking isn't usual at either business or social gatherings, so limit your alcohol intake to a social amount. And finally, don't forget to say *adiós* and *gracias* to your hosts before leaving.

BE MY GUEST

Entertaining at home is purely social. Even if your host or guests are business colleagues, business is not discussed. Prepare yourself for conversations about sports, family, international events, and so on. If you show up at the designated hour, you will probably catch the host and hostess in the final stages of preparation, so plan to arrive at least a half an hour later. Don't expect that dinner will be served immediately, but do expect to stick around after the meal for conversation.

Your attire for a dinner invitation to a colleague's home will depend on where you are, the people involved, and the nature of the get-together. Generally speaking, these events tend to be slightly formal, requiring a suit and tie for men and a dress for women. You can ask your host or hostess if you are unsure, and if you have any lingering doubts, it's better to err on the side of dressing up than dressing down.

Etiquette calls for you to arrive with a hostess gift. This could be a box of chocolates, a bottle of top quality wine or liquor, or a coffee-table book. In most of Central America, flowers are inexpensive and plentiful, and as such are not a good hostess gift. White flowers are uplifting, but red ones are associated with casting evil spells, and yellow ones connote death. Avoid marigolds, which are used to decorate graves.

If you are invited to stay with a family for a more extended period, you will also want to bring a gift or two appropriate to the family. This might be a CD, some books or small toys for the children, or a gift for the house. Many middle- and upper-class families have a maid or other household help. If your hosts do, respect the roles that employer and employee play. For example, do not offer to help clear the table or wash the dishes if there is a maid. Most ladies of the house would not like to have you tip their maids, but if you are there for an extended stay or if the maid performs some special service for you, such as doing your laundry, you might want to ask your hostess if you may give her a token gift to show your appreciation.

DINING ETIQUETTE POINTERS

Keep both hands above the table at all times, but not with your elbows on the table. Unlike Americans, Central Americans generally do not switch their forks between hands. The fork remains in the left hand and the knife in the right hand. Luckily, mastering this also means that you will find it easier to keep your hands above the table!

As we've mentioned before, many middle- and upper-class families have household help, so meals may be served by a maid. The maid may place platters on the table at a more informal meal or serve each person individually for a more formal occasion.

Men should be prepared with a toast, especially if hosting the meal. If possible, offer the toast in Spanish. An amusing anecdote or story wouldn't be amiss here either. Women generally do not offer toasts.

DINING OUT

If you are invited to a restaurant, be punctual, especially if reservations have been made.

Restaurant checks are generally not divided; one person pays for the group. A little good-natured battling over who gets to pay the bill is common, with the host winning. If you are the guest, you should insist that your host allow you to invite him as your guest at a later date. Tipping customs vary from country to country. Please see the Tipping section for each country.

HEALTH

Health is usually a major concern for those moving to Central America, especially since tales of Montezuma's Revenge abound. While it will certainly take time for your system to adjust to the local environment, there are ways to stave off serious illness. One of the easiest ways to ease your system into sync is to watch what you eat and drink. Although the local residents may drink tap water, it is preferable to use bottled or filtered water. It is also a good idea to use filtered water to wash fruits and vegetables and for making ice cubes. Many expatriates have found it most helpful to arrange to have a filter installed into their home water supply to eliminate the inconvenience of using bottled water. In addition, the American water system is supplemented with fluoride; the water in Central America is not. Consider asking your dentist if you need a substitute fluoride treatment, especially if you are moving with children.

Although medicines are readily available in most major cities in Central America, consider taking a few months' supply of any prescription medicine to give you time to find a doctor. Have your doctor provide the generic names for any prescription medication in case a particular brand is not available. Please note, however, that you must be very careful about taking any kind of medicine, prescription or over-the-counter, into many Central American countries, as many countries are very sensitive about drugs. Be sure everything is in its original container and is very clearly marked. If your medication is a narcotic, it can also be helpful to have a letter explaining why you need that particular medication. In most places, pharmacies rotate the responsibility of being available for emergencies during off hours.

FOCUS: MEXICO

HOUSING

Both unfurnished and furnished housing are available. You can expect to sign a one-year lease, although you may be able to negotiate a shorter term if necessary. An advance of one month's rent (two months' rent for a furnished apartment) and a security deposit are standard requirements to secure your home. Many rental properties have an additional charge for security services, and newer apartment

buildings may have a monthly maintenance fee. There will be no fee paid to the real-estate agent who locates your home; that fee is paid by the landlord. You may need a co-signer on a lease as a guarantor. Try to verify that the previous tenants didn't leave any unpaid rent or utility bills, which can be a big headache to straighten out.

Be sure that the landlord is registered with the federal tax bureau. Only these landlords (i.e., those who are paying taxes on the income from the rental) are able to issue an official receipt (*factura*), an item you will need if you are claiming all or part of the cost of the apartment as a business expense.

Heating and air-conditioning are considered luxuries in Mexico. Do not assume that your new place will come with either. Water shortages are a problem in some areas. Find out what measures have been taken in your new home to combat the problem. If there is a cistern on the roof, be sure to check on its condition.

Having a new telephone line installed can be time consuming. It is far better if your new home already has one. If it does not, you will need to go to the Telmex office nearest you and fill out an application. Installation can take a week or it can take up to four months. You can request a copy of the current telephone directory at the local Telmex office when you apply or when you first move in. Thereafter you can expect to receive an updated version automatically.

You will need to go to the appropriate offices to have the utilities changed over into your name. Be sure you take along proof of your residence (i.e., the lease) and photo I.D. Don't be surprised if it takes a couple of trips to get things straightened out.

And finally, Mexico has experienced devastating earthquakes in the past few years. It's important to find out as much as you can about the structural soundness of your building, especially in high-rises.

HEALTH

Doctors abound in Mexico, and medical care is moderately priced. Medical care is available at low cost through the *Instituto Mexicano*

de Seguro Social, the Mexican Social Security system, which has a network of clinics and hospitals. Anyone residing in Mexico can participate in the public system, although most expatriates prefer to use private services to avoid the frustrations of the long lines and delays that are sometimes encountered in the public system.

In addition to social security, one can obtain private medical insurance through one's employer or individually. There are numerous private hospitals and clinics, especially in Mexico's largest cities. The best way to find a physician or hospital is to ask friends and colleagues for recommendations. Many doctors make house calls, though there is an additional charge. This can be especially helpful for families with children.

And while we're on the topic of health, it's important to note that air pollution is a serious problem in Mexico City and Guadalajara, and is increasingly problematic in Monterrey. Air-quality readings are published daily in the newspapers; a reading above 150 points is considered harmful. When the air-pollution counts are high, it is advisable to stay indoors as much as possible and to avoid strenuous exercise. You can get an air purifier to help reduce contaminates in your home.

SHOPPING

Mexico's major cities offer a wide variety of places to shop, from open-air markets to sophisticated shopping malls. A wide variety of both domestic and imported goods is available in larger cities. Markets are where you can find fresh fruits and vegetables, flowers, local handicrafts, and more. This is where you can use your bargaining skills to get the best prices.

MONEY AND BANKING

Mexico has several large banks with branches throughout the country, as well as smaller banks and branches of many international

banks. Service and convenience have improved since Mexico began privatizing the banking industry in the early 1990s.

Checks are widely accepted in major cities and can be used to purchase groceries and household items in larger stores and to pay your monthly bills. Keep in mind, however, that smaller shops may not accept a check.

When you open your account, you may be asked to provide information about your employment, including your employer's business registration number (*cédula*) and job description. Depending on the type of permit you hold, your employer might need to write a letter of recommendation to the bank.

Credit cards are becoming more popular in Mexico, but have not reached the same currency as they have in the United States. You can expect that larger hotels and stores will accept credit cards; smaller businesses may not. Most of the major Mexican banks now offer a bank credit card. If you are interested in obtaining one of these, be sure you first find out how widely accepted it is. Keep in mind that Mexican interest rates are comparably higher than those in the United States. ATMs are widely available in major cities.

The Mexican currency is the peso, indicated by $, N$ or N.P. (*nuevo peso*), or M.N. (*Moneda Nacional*); there are 100 centavos (¢) in a peso. Notes are in denominations of N$100, N$50, N$20, and N$10; coins are in denominations of N$10, N$5, N$1, 50¢, 20¢, 10¢, and 5¢. Several years ago, the government printed new currency as part of its economic reform program, dropping three zeros from each denomination. Some of the old bills are still in circulation and are interchangeable with the new currency.

Bank hours at many branches are quite short, usually from 9:00 A.M. to 2:30 P.M. Some branches reopen from 4:00 to 6:00 P.M. and/or on weekends. ATMs have increased in number exponentially in recent years and are widely available in major cities. Some banks' ATMs are part of the Cirrus or Plus systems, which will allow you to use a debit card from your home account. Some machines dispense either Mexican pesos or U.S. dollars.

Credit cards are widely accepted, especially in hotels and larger stores. Visa and MasterCard are the most popular, American Express somewhat less so. When you check into a hotel, you may be asked to sign a blank credit-card slip to cover incidental expenses; this is a normal practice.

American Express has offices in many Mexican cities. If you have an American Express card, you can cash a personal check drawn on a foreign account and take advantage of other services.

A 15% VAT (Value Added Tax) applies to all purchases. The price listed usually includes the VAT.

Tipping

Tipping is not very common in Mexico. However, many people have come to expect tips from foreigners, especially in Mexico City. While it is fine to leave a generous tip, arrogantly throwing money around is unlikely to earn you either respect or better service. You can tip in U.S. dollars in many places. Following are a few guidelines for tipping:

- If the service is not included in the restaurant bill, tip 10–15%.
- Porters/bellboys can be tipped about 10–20 pesos per bag, or the current equivalent of $2.
- In a hotel, leave an optional 10–20 pesos per day, or the current equivalent of $2, for the maid.
- Tip the room-service waiter 10–20 pesos, or the current equivalent of $2.
- Taxi drivers are tipped about 10% of the fare. This is not expected, so it's optional.
- Americans are generally not used to tipping gas-station attendants; in Mexico, tip 5–10 pesos, or the current equivalent of $1–2.
- If there is a rest-room attendant, leave a small tip of 5–10 pesos, or the current equivalent of $1.

TELEPHONES

Public telephones are easily found on the streets of most larger cities, although they don't always work. The telephones marked Lada (for *Larga Distancia*, or long distance) can be used for local calls as well.

Mexican telephones come in a confusing array of colors and styles. Older phones only take peso coins. Most newer phones accept coins, telephone cards, Mexican bank cards, major credit cards, or a combination.

Most public telephones in urban areas now take telephone cards (*tarjetas telefónicas* or *tarjetas Ladatel*). The cards have values of 25, 50 or 100 pesos and can be purchased at news kiosks and many shops, which usually display a blue and yellow sign reading *De Venta Aquí Ladatel*. The display on the telephone will tell you how much is left on your card.

You can also make calls at a *caseta de teléfono*. You will pay a heavy surcharge, but will not have to use a phone card and casetas are generally more quiet than a street corner.

You can usually use your American or Canadian calling card in Mexico, but contact your service provider to find out what the proper procedures are.

Useful Numbers

Mexico City: 06 for all emergencies. Although many emergency operators speak English, if you are having language difficulties, you can call SECTUR, a special assistance hotline for tourists. They have many numbers in Mexico City, including 5/250–0123, 5/250–0493, and 5/250–0027.

Guadalajara: 080 for all emergencies.
Oaxaca: 060 for all emergencies.

FOCUS: BELIZE

MONEY AND BANKING

The Belizean currency is the dollar, which is divided into 100 cents. Bills are in denominations of 100, 20, 10, 5, and 1 dollars. Coins are in denominations of 50, 25, 10, 5, and 1 cents.

U.S. currency is accepted in many places. Prices are sometimes listed in both U.S. and Belizean dollars. Credit cards are accepted at larger hotels and stores. However, there may be an additional charge for using one.

Tipping

Note: The following amounts are in Belizean dollars.

- Tipping at restaurants is optional, although a 10–15% tip is expected in hotel restaurants.
- Taxi drivers aren't tipped unless they perform an extra service, such as carrying your baggage. In that case, $1–2 is appropriate.
- $1 or $2 is an appropriate amount for bellboys or porters who carry your bags.

- If you take a guided tour, tip the guide $2–3 per person in your group.

TELEPHONES

Pay phones are hard to find outside Belize City. The cost of a call is 25 cents (Belizean) for three minutes. Phones may take either coins or phone cards. To make a call—local, long distance, or international—you can go to the local BTL (Belize Telecommunications Ltd.) office.

Useful Numbers[1]

Police: 911
Ambulance: 90
International operator: 115

DRESS

Jeans are fine for casual wear. More formal occasions call for a business suit for men and a nice dress for women. You can leave your tuxedo at home. Women should avoid short shorts and provocative clothing in general.

MISCELLANEOUS

Dropping by someone's home is not considered rude, especially since many people do not have phones. If you know your Belizean friend has a telephone, it's nice to call ahead as a courtesy (and to see if he or she is home!).

[1] As these numbers may have changed over the past years, it would be advisable to look them up in the yellow pages when you arrive. They appear prominently on the first pages.

Hostess gifts are not expected, but are a nice gesture. You can bring wine or a dessert if you are invited to someone's home.

Avoid people who approach you offering their services as a guide. If you are interested in a tour, you can contact the Belize Tourist Office or ask at a reputable hotel.

FOCUS: COSTA RICA

HOUSING

Rental leases are generally for a term of three years unless stated otherwise in the rental contract. Landlords are limited to a 15% increase in rent per year.

Having telephone service connected can be difficult. Even if lines are available in your area, it can take several months before you get connected. If possible, try to take over the line from the previous tenant.

Part-time or full-time (live-in) domestic help is widely available and relatively inexpensive. The Labor Code applies to domestic employees, so there is usually no written contract for these services. If you desire a written contract, you will need to observe the relevant articles in the Code.

Local television programming is exclusively in Spanish. However, with cable or a satellite dish you will be able to access many U.S. stations. Several radio stations broadcast in English.

SHOPPING

Every town and neighborhood has a *pulpería*, or corner grocery. Supermarkets are available in larger cities, and the number of malls is growing every year. Imported goods are available in larger stores, but are usually quite expensive due to import duties.

When you have selected something to buy in a department store, you will be given an invoice, which you take to the cashier to pay. You must then proceed to a separate counter to pick up your merchandise. The concept of self-service is growing in Costa Rica, but is by no means common. In many smaller stores you must request what you want from the person manning the counter.

MONEY AND BANKING

Costa Rica's unit of currency is the colón (¢), with one hundred céntimos equaling one colón. Bills are in denominations of 10,000, 5,000, 2,000, 1,000, 500, 100, and 50 colones. There are both silver and gold coins. These are in denominations of 20, 10, 5, 2, and 1 céntimos (silver) and 100, 50, 25, 10, and 5 céntimos (gold).

Most banks have ATMs that accept Cirrus, Plus, MasterCard, Visa, and American Express. You may have a choice of receiving colones or dollars. Money can be exchanged at banks, hotels, and *casas de cambio* (exchange offices). Rates are likely to be more favorable at the latter; hotels usually have the worst rates. It is not advisable to change money on the street, even though you may be offered attractive rates. In addition to its being illegal, you are likely to receive counterfeit bills.

Banks are usually open from 9:00 A.M. to 3:00 P.M. Monday through Friday. Some branches offer extended hours on certain days and/or weekend hours.

Personal Banking

Need to catch up on your reading? You will have plenty of time as you stand in line at the bank. Although things are changing, most banks lack modern equipment and are plagued with long lines. You will have to grin and bear it; complaining will do you no good. Be sure you get in the correct line. Most banks have separate lines for deposits, check cashing, etc. If you don't know which line to stand in, ask two or more people to be sure you're in the right line. Workers are paid on the 15th and 30th of the month; try to plan your banking around those dates if possible.

Many banks offer accounts in either dollars or colones. Colón accounts usually have a higher interest rate to compensate for devaluation against the dollar. The Central Bank sets the official exchange rate, devaluing by 10 to 12 céntimos daily.

In order to open a checking account, you must be a resident of Costa Rica. You will also need a recommendation from two individuals with accounts at that bank. Your company can probably help by writing a letter of recommendation. Be sure to take your passport and an initial deposit to open the account. Funds deposited in the three autonomous state banks (Banco Nacional de Costa Rica, Banco de Costa Rica, Banco de Crédito Agrícola de Cartago) are guaranteed by the government.

You can open an account at a *casa de cambio* (exchange office), which will allow you to cash personal checks without the hassles of a bank. Just make sure the establishment is registered with SUGEF; otherwise it is illegal.

Most banks have ATMs linked to the Cirrus and Plus systems, allowing you to withdraw from your U.S. account, assuming your home bank is also part of one of these networks. You can also get cash advances from your Visa, MasterCard, or American Express card. Many machines will give you either colones or dollars.

You can pay your utility and telephone bills at a local ICE (Costa Rican Electricity Institute) branch or in certain banks and supermarkets. No bill will arrive the mail; the utility company sends messengers to collect payment.

Tipping

A 10% service charge is already included in your bill at restaurants. Additional tipping is not necessary, but you may tip if you wish.

If you are staying at a private home and the maid performs some service for you, such as doing your laundry, it is nice to tip her ¢200–¢500. In a hotel, tipping the maid is at your discretion.

Parking-lot attendants are not tipped unless they perform a special service. However, if you park on the street, you will inevitably be approached by someone offering to "guard" your car for you. It is best to accept and tip ¢50–¢200 when you return to your car.

If the boy at the supermarket takes your groceries out to your car, tip him ¢50–¢100.

A porter or bellhop should get about 30–40 colones per bag.

Gas-station attendants are tipped 5–10 colones.

TELEPHONES

Public phones may take coins or phone cards. International calls can be made from private or public phones.

Useful Numbers

International operator: 116
Emergency: 911
Police: 117
Rural Police: 127
Fire Department: 118

FOCUS: EL SALVADOR

MONEY AND BANKING

El Salvador's currency is the colón (¢). There are 100 centavos in a colón; coins are issued in denominations of 50, 25, 10, 5, and 1 centavos. There are two different series of coins, so two coins of the same value may have a different size, which can be disorienting. Bills are in denominations of 100, 50, 25, 10, and 5 colones.

The Salvadoran currency is not widely exchangeable outside El Salvador, so you may want to change your money to another currency before leaving the country.

You can change money at banks or *casas de cambio*. El Salvador is a cash society; you will find it difficult to change traveler's checks. Make room in your wallet by leaving your credit cards at home.

TELEPHONES

ANTEL, El Salvador's state-owned telecommunications company, was split in 1998 into two companies: CTE (Corporación de Telecomunicaciones de El Salvador) for land lines and Intelsa for the cellular network. Several companies offer telephone service since the market opened to competition. When you make a long-distance or international call, you will need to first enter the access code of the service you wish to use. You can check local newspapers for advertisements to find the most competitive rates and the corresponding codes if you are inclined to do a little comparison shopping.

A local call will cost you 75 centavos for three minutes. There are public phones that accept coins and phones that accept cards. If you are out and about, you can make international calls and send faxes and telexes at CTE.

Useful Numbers

Information: 114 (English is spoken)
Long-distance information, collect calls within El Salvador: 110
Police: 121
Fire (San Salvador): 2712227
Hospital (San Salvador): 2254481

FOCUS: GUATEMALA

MONEY AND BANKING

Guatemala's currency is the quetzal, equal to 100 centavos. Bills are in denominations of 100, 50, 20, 10, 5, and 1 quetzales; coins are in denominations of 25, 10, 5, and 1 centavos.

Cash is the way to go in Guatemala. However, major credit cards are accepted in larger hotels, stores, and restaurants. You may not be able to use one in smaller establishments. U.S. dollar traveler's checks can be cashed in most major Guatemala City banks. Outside the capital it is more difficult to find a bank to cash your traveler's checks; try the Banco de Guatemala branch in the department's major city. U.S. dollars are the easiest foreign currency to exchange; other currencies, including those of other Central American countries, can be virtually impossible to exchange, especially outside Guatemala City. If you need to exchange non-U.S. currency, your best bet is the exchange office at the airport. It's a good idea to keep smaller bills and coins on hand so as to be able to use exact change.

Although hours can vary, most banks are open from 9:00 A.M. until 6:00 P.M. Monday to Friday and until 1:00 P.M. on Saturdays.

Tipping

The service charge is not included in the meal. Leave a tip of about 10%. If you are eating in a small family-run restaurant, tipping is optional, but most people leave at least some change.

Give the hotel porter who helps you with your bag a quetzal; if you stay for a few days, leave a couple of quetzales for the maid.

It is not necessary to tip the taxi driver once you have negotiated the fare.

Yo Quiero....Moo Goo Gai Pan?

Most people think of rice, tortillas, and beans when they think of Central American cuisine. But when you are in Guatemala, you will probably notice a surprising number of Chinese restaurants. They can offer a change of pace at a reasonable price, but don't expect the food to taste the same as it did at home—or in China, for that matter—since it has been adapted to the local environment.

TELEPHONES

Both local and domestic long-distance calls are quite inexpensive, but international calls are extraordinarily expensive. International and long-distance calls can be made from the local office of Guatel, Guatemala's telephone company. All calls have a three-minute minimum. Pay phones accept 10 and 25 centavo coins; a local call costs 10 centavos. If your call will be more than three minutes, deposit several extra coins. If you haven't, you will be cut off. Extra change will be returned at the end of the call. Public telephones are available only in larger cities. The best place to find a phone is in front of the Guatel office or in the lobbies of larger hotels and pharmacies. If the pay phone you are using has a button on the phone box beneath the handset, you will need to push the button when your call is answered so that the other person can hear you.

Useful Numbers

Police: 110
Operator-assisted International Calls: 171
Directory Assistance: 124
Fire: 122 or 123

POST OFFICE

In Guatemala City, the main post office is open weekdays from 8:00 A.M. to 6:00 P.M., and from 8:00 A.M. to noon on Saturdays. Hours are shorter outside Guatemala City; most local post-office branches close at 4:30 P.M. While both domestic and international postal rates are quite inexpensive, the mail service is unreliable.

It is not advisable to send anything of value through the mail system. Instead, try a courier service. FedEx, UPS, and DHL all have offices in Guatemala City and Antigua. Service at the post office varies, and you may find yourself at the whim of the local postal agent. If you want to send a package from Guatemala, be prepared to unwrap it if the postal agent wants to inspect the contents.

FOCUS: HONDURAS

HEALTH AND SAFETY

Pharmacies are readily available. Many items that are available only with a prescription in the United States, such as antibiotics, can be bought over the counter. Drugs that do require a prescription are quite inexpensive.

Honduran medical facilities, while not as modern as those in the U.S., are adequate and medical personnel are very capable. The quality of medical care is quite high.

Mosquitoes and "no-see-ums" abound in some parts; take plenty of insect repellent with you. While no vaccinations are necessary for entry into the country, you may want to check with your doctor for advice before traveling to Honduras.

Intestinal problems from ingesting tap water are a very real issue. Stick to bottled water and avoid ice cubes made with tap water and fruits and vegetables washed in tap water. If you will be living in Honduras, you will probably want to explore your options for a filtration system in your home.

Crime, while not frequent, has increased in recent years. There have been incidences of armed muggings and robbery, but on the whole most people feel safe while visiting.

MONEY AND BANKING

The colorful Honduran currency, the lempira, comes in denominations of 100 (orange), 50 (blue), 20 (green), 10 (black), 5 (brown), and 1 lempiras (red). Coins, called centavos, are infrequent, but you may see 50- and 20-centavo pieces. Your U.S. ATM cards will probably not be compatible with a Honduran ATM, if you are even able to find one. Keep some U.S. currency on hand, especially small bills. Many places such as hotels and restaurants will accept it in a pinch. It can also be handy for the occasional "gift" to an official.

Credit cards are accepted in some places such as hotels and larger restaurants; otherwise expect to use cash. You may be charged a surcharge when you pay with a credit card.

Tipping

Hondurans do not generally tip, although a tip is often expected from foreigners.

Taxi drivers are not tipped unless they carry baggage or perform some other special service.

Tip about half what you would tip in the United States.

TELEPHONES

Honduras has the lowest number of telephones per capita in Central America, only about two and a half phones per 100 people. Most towns have a Hondutel office, the Honduran telephone company, where you can make a telephone call if you can't locate a phone elsewhere. You can probably make a call from a hotel, even if you aren't a guest, although there may be a surcharge.

Useful Numbers

Information: 192
Fire: 198
Police: 199

POST OFFICE

Post offices are open from 7:00 A.M. to 6:00 P.M. Monday through Friday and from 8:00 A.M. to noon on Saturday. Mail service is uneven. For important packages, it's better to use a courier service. UPS, FedEx, Airborne, and other shippers operate in Honduras.

FOCUS: NICARAGUA

MONEY AND BANKING

The Nicaraguan unit of currency is the córdoba, which is divided into 100 centavos. Bills are in denominations of 100, 50, 20, 10, 5, and 1 córdobas and 25 and 10 centavos. Coins are in 25, 20, 10, and 5 centavos.

Nicaragua's currency has been stable for several years; the days of astronomical inflation are past. While you may encounter some prices in U.S. dollars, which were used during the inflationary period, you can pay in córdobas. U.S. dollars can be exchanged at banks or at *casas de cambio*; if you are carrying Canadian dollars or other foreign currencies, you may run into difficulty finding a place to change it. Traveler's checks can be difficult to cash; you will probably have better luck at a *casa de cambio* than at a bank. You can use your Visa or MasterCard in better hotels and restaurants in most places.

Tipping

- Tip porters $0.50 per bag.
- Taxi drivers do not receive a tip.
- You can leave up to 10% in nice restaurants.

TELEPHONES

All telephone lines in Nicaragua are owned by Empresa Nicaragüense de Telecomunicaciones (Enitel). Public phones may take coins or cards. Long-distance or international calls can be made from private or public phones; if you can't find one, you can go to the nearest Enitel office.

FOCUS: PANAMA

HOUSING

Housing in Panama is relatively easy to find, thanks to the building boom of the early 1990s. Both homes and apartments are available for rent. Housing in furnished apartments and residence hotels is also available in Panama City, and may be preferable to signing a lease for someone staying for the short to medium term.

Newer buildings and complexes provide greater amenities, and are priced accordingly. Many larger homes and luxury apartments have a maid's quarters attached, as most upper-class people have a live-in maid.

When you decide on a house or apartment to rent, you and the landlord will sign a lease, which is then filed with the Ministry of Housing in Panama City. A security deposit is also required by the landlord; however, any rental fees from the real-estate agency are usually paid by the landlord.

You will need to arrange to have the utilities reconnected. You can contact the local gas and electricity company for information, but you will probably need to appear in person to take care of the connection. Your water service will probably be arranged by the landlord, but you should be sure to ask who pays for it. Telephone-line installation can take several weeks if your home does not already

have service, so be sure you inquire if the home or apartment has a
phone line. You will need to visit the telephone company in person
to sign up for service and pay a fee. Note that although your bills for
utilities and telephone should come by mail, you are responsible for
paying them even if the bill doesn't arrive. Non-payment is likely to
result in termination of service, even if you didn't receive a bill. If
you have any questions, call or go to the appropriate office.

HEALTH AND SAFETY

Panama is one of Central America's most dangerous countries;
Colón is particularly dangerous. Use extra caution and your common sense. Don't wear expensive jewelry and avoid walking after
dark. Women should not go about unaccompanied and should be
careful of purse snatchers.

MONEY AND BANKING

Panama uses U.S. banknotes, called Balboas, but has its own coins
in denominations of 10 Balboas, 50, 25, 10, 5, and 1 cents. The 50-
cent piece is called a peso and the 5-cent piece is called a real. Coins
are used interchangeably with U.S. coins. Credit cards are widely
accepted in Panama City and in larger hotels and restaurants in
other areas.

Tipping

- Porters and bellhops who carry your bags should get about $1
  per bag.
- Taxi drivers receive about a 10% tip.
- A service charge is not included in your restaurant bill. Add a
  10–15% tip.
- If the gas-station attendant washes your windshield, checks
  your oil, etc., tip him 25–50¢.

- If you are staying in someone's home for several days, you can discreetly tip the maid (if there is one) $5 or so, especially if she has done something special for you, such as doing your laundry.

TELEPHONES

Telephone service in Panama is operated by the British Cable & Wireless Corporation. Cellular service is through C&W and Bell South.

You can make calls within Panama from any coin-operated public phone, located on major streets. There are a couple of different types of phones, so read the instructions. Some phones require you to deposit a coin first, others have you dial the number and then deposit the coins at the recorded prompting when the phone has been picked up on the other end.

If you need to make a long-distance or collect call, you can go to an office of ENTEL (Panama's telephone company).

Useful Numbers

International operator: 106
Police: 104
Fire: 103
Ambulance: 269–9778

SIX

BUSINESS ENVIRONMENT IN MEXICO AND CENTRAL AMERICA

Vísteme despacio, que llevo prisa.

I'm in a hurry, dress me slowly.

WORK ETHIC

One of the most common negative stereotypes many Americans hold about Central Americans is that they are lazy. In fact, many people, especially those who are not white-collar workers, work six days a week. It is more likely that the label arose not from any inherent laziness in the people of Central America, but from a combination of cultural differences.

Time. As mentioned in earlier sections, Central Americans have a much more flexible approach toward time. To someone who sees schedules and deadlines as absolutes, it can appear that Central Americans just aren't willing to do the work it takes to stick to the schedule, and lack discipline.

Priorities. For most Central Americans, family takes precedence over work. There is a strong familial bond and a corresponding sense of obligation to the family. This impacts the work world in many ways. People take time off from work for family events such as weddings, first communions, graduations, and funerals, as well as for a sickness in the family. Holidays are stretched as much as possible. If a holiday falls on a Thursday or Tuesday, the intervening Friday or Monday may be taken off to extend the holiday. These *puentes* (bridges) can be one day or several days; whatever it takes to make the most of consecutive holidays.

Philosophy. One of the important truths to remember about working in Central America is that while Americans live to work, Central Americans work to live. Americans have the tendency to view work almost as their raison d'être, and it is the central focus of their lives. Most people in Central America, on the other hand, view work as a necessary evil. Their lives outside of work are what is important in the final analysis.

A Dios rogando y con el mazo dando.
Pray to God and hammer away.

Fatalism. Fatalism is a part of Central American cultures and can have a direct impact on the work environment. If the inherent belief that one does not have control over one's fate is reinforced by a work environment where the worker feels that his skills are unappreciated and his initiative is unrewarded, he is likely to believe that the tasks he performs are unimportant. This situation can be corrected by fostering an atmosphere in which workers are respected and valued, and where initiative is rewarded, which will increase employee loyalty and effort.

ETHICS AND BRIBERY

La mordida (the bite) or bribery is a fact of business life in Central America, although it is becoming less common in some countries. Some of the most commonly told tales of bribery solicitation have to do with customs officials. Because these officials have the ability to delay, or even confiscate, the goods that pass across their country's borders, they are in a powerful position. Civic employees have also been known to expedite paperwork or cut through red tape when presented with a "gift," and policemen to issue a warning instead of a speeding ticket when discreetly slipped a few bills. Presidents and other high-level administrators have even left office with heavy pockets thanks to their ability to influence the awarding of government contracts.

If the idea of bribery is foreign, or even repulsive, to you, there are some things you should take into consideration. Bribery tends to bring to mind the image of some fat cat looking to further line his pockets. While this is sometimes the case, as cited above in the example of highly placed individuals peddling their influence, it is not usually greed that inspires *la mordida*. Wages throughout Central America are generally low, making it difficult for people to support their families. Those in a position to do so may take advantage of an opportunity to supplement their income.

Keep in mind, too, that you do not have to pay a bribe, even if one is suggested. Many companies have policies pertaining to bribery. It is important that you know what your company's guidelines are before you venture into Central America. You will have to weigh the potential impact of your action, your company's policy, and your own degree of comfort with the practice of bribery. If you are shipping canned tuna, it may not matter if it is delayed a few weeks in customs; if you are shipping eggs, it's a different matter altogether.

Before you condemn the practice of bribery, remember that many people in Central America abhor it as well. However, they view it is a necessary evil in the face of low salaries.

PERSONAL SPACE

Central Americans and Americans are at odds over many things. Personal space is one area where we are different. Trivial as it may seem, it can be an important, albeit unconscious, part of our assessment of each other. If you were to watch two Americans having a conversation, you would note that they keep each other at arm's length—literally. Americans are most comfortable when the other person is about three feet away from them. Any closer and one feels encroached upon. Central Americans, on the other hand, have a much smaller bubble of personal space. A matter of inches, you might say, but those inches have repercussions. The Central American tries to close the space while the American backs up, making for an interesting dance around the room, but creating discomfort for both parties, even if the reason isn't on the surface of either party's mind.

Closely related to personal space is the use—or lack thereof—of touching. Central Americans in general touch more than Americans, especially in a business setting. In the United States, touching is largely limited to handshakes, perhaps a hearty clap on the back. Throughout Central America, on the other hand, you will find that people use touching as an integral part of communication. Handshakes are called for in business, certainly, but it is common to see people embracing or kissing, if they are of opposite genders, in greeting, even in a business environment. Even handshaking protocol is different. Handshakes tend to be warmer and longer, and are generally more frequent. Physical contact continues throughout the conversation; your partner may touch your arm or throw his arm around your shoulders in camaraderie.

Americans tend to find the Central American style of personal interaction difficult to handle to varying degrees, especially if the people involved are of opposite genders. The typical Central American level of contact in an American environment would indicate an intimate relationship or inappropriate behavior. It should be stressed that there is a clear distinction between normal interaction and sexual harassment. Women who use their common sense quickly learn the norms and are able to ascertain whether those boundaries have been breached.

The best advice is to try to bring the reasons for your discomfort to your consciousness and try to simply go with the flow. After a while, you will become accustomed to it and will adapt.

COMPETITION

Americans are notoriously competitive, a cultural trait that most Central Americans lack, and one that is out of place in most Central American organizations. As stated earlier, the path to the top has little to do with one's accomplishments and much to do with who one knows. In addition, Central Americans would rather avoid open conflict, as indicated by their reluctance to say "no" outright, and place more value than Americans in maintaining dignity, which would be destroyed in a fiercely competitive environment. The competitive environment is therefore ineffective, and a relaxed, friendly atmosphere is preferred.

This doesn't mean, of course, that Central Americans sit shyly in the corner and prefer anonymity. On the contrary, recognition for outstanding work can be a powerful motivator, as long as it was not achieved at the expense of a colleague.

THE OFFICE HIERARCHY

The office hierarchy is not to be ignored in Central America. Americans have a habit of doing whatever it takes to get something done. This means that if one needs a piece of information from another department, one simply asks. It's also acceptable in most instances to go directly to the source or to the decision-maker, as long as one keeps the appropriate people "in the loop." Trying this approach in Central America is a sure-fire way to make yourself an enemy. Status and authority are valued; threatening that will net you nothing but trouble.

The key to getting things done, as usual, is relationships. You will want to establish a network, preferably including people in the right positions to facilitate your business. Trying to jump ranks in your own company will not serve you in the long run, even if it accomplishes your immediate goal, as it will give you a reputation as untrustworthy. Going over someone's head outside your company will earn you the ill will of the person slighted, and could come back to haunt you when that person places hurdles in your way in the future. In short, you cannot be a bull in a china shop and expect to succeed in the long run. You will have to play by the rules.

FAMILY AND RELIGION

Families are an important part of life in Central America. As stated earlier, most people in Central America work to live, and family obligations take priority over work. This means that someone on your team may feel that it's more important for him to attend his cousin's wedding than a negotiation that you see as critical to your company. By the same token, they would probably wonder at your priorities if you were to skip the wedding in favor of attending the meeting.

Americans, with their tradition of separation of church and state, find it difficult to understand the role that religion plays in the lives of most Central Americans. With the exception of Belize, all Central American countries are over 75% Roman Catholic; most, in fact, are over 95% Roman Catholic. Belize has the lowest Catholic population, but even there 65% of the population is Catholic.

This obviously does not mean that every person in Central America goes to church every Sunday. Most, however, do observe the religious rituals and milestones throughout their life, and many businesses consider religion to be a uniting force. The most obvious influence on business is the holiday schedule, which reflects Catholic holidays in most countries. However, it's not unusual to see religious images in the workplace or to have a priest bless a newly built office or plant or even hold a special mass for employees and their families.

BUSINESS PROTOCOL

The Central American business environment is overall more formal than that of the United States. This is reflected in many ways, including the importance of following proper protocol, the way one dresses for business, the use of language, and so forth.

Business Cards

Business cards are a very important part of doing business in Central America. Aside from providing details such as your address and telephone number, they help to establish your place within the organization and thus your status and level of responsibility. Clues to your importance lie in your job title, the type of degree you hold, and even your family name, all of which are printed on your card.

If possible, have your card printed in Spanish on one side. Make

sure your title reflects your level of responsibility accurately. This is especially important if you will be interacting with high-level Central Americans or have been given leadership responsibilities. If your current title is not on a par with those of the people with whom you need to do business, it might be a good idea to request that your company give you a more important title, even if only temporarily. List any degrees you hold over the level of a bachelor's degree, using the Spanish equivalent if possible.

Dressing for Success

Being well groomed is important to most Central American businesspeople. The focus is on dressing appropriately, not the cost of the clothing. As a general rule, Central Americans dress up rather than down.

Men should stick to the classic business suit. Darker colors are more prevalent, although lighter colors are perfectly acceptable. In hotter weather, Central American men may wear a *guayabera* and slacks in lieu of a suit. The *guayabera* is a lightweight, loose shirt, usually white with an open neck, which is worn outside the trousers. Dressier versions have intricate embroidery. Most foreign businessmen find that it is generally better to stick to one's own business attire rather than appropriating the native style of dress.

Women can wear a suit or dress. High heels and hose are expected in most places, even on the hottest days. While you may see some secretaries wearing miniskirts, it is not appropriate for managers and executives. Most businesswomen are well coifed, manicured, and made up. It is fine if you prefer not to use the heavy makeup favored by most women, but you should always look well groomed. Both men and women wear more jewelry than in the United States.

If you are going to a business social event, you can always ask a colleague for advice on the appropriate attire if you are unsure. Managers are generally expected to dress and act the part.

Greetings and Conversation

The handshake is the common greeting in business, although men may greet each other with an *abrazo* (hug) if they know each other. A woman should extend her hand first for a handshake. Women who know each other may greet with a kiss (or kisses) on the cheek. A man greeting a woman he knows well may kiss her cheek or combine a handshake with a kiss. When kissing in greeting, the kiss is usually an air kiss with the cheeks touching, not a big smack on the cheek.

Handshakes are usually more extended than in the United States. They can be double-handed and can last a lot longer than you are probably used to at home. Again, don't pull away. Handshakes, kisses, and the like happen more often than you may expect. You will find yourself shaking hands with friends and colleagues almost every time you see them, regardless of how long it has been since

your last meeting. You will shake hands when taking your leave as well as upon meeting.

You must get comfortable with more physical contact in greeting and in general. If you, like many foreigners, are confused by the protocol, the best approach is to be prepared for anything, but to let your counterpart initiate any contact beyond a handshake. Do *not* pull away from a hug or kiss.

Once the initial hellos are shared, it's time for conversation. You can probably guess that good ice-breaker topics of conversation include children, travel, local sites, etc. Politics, religion, race, illegal immigration, and other sensitive topics are best avoided.

If you're going to be conversing and building relationships in Spanish, remember that you should always begin your relationships by using *Usted*, the formal version of "you" to show your respect. If a close personal relationship develops, your colleague may suggest moving to *tu*; let him or her initiate the transition to informal address.

Titles are very important; be sure to use them. Some common titles are *Doctor(a)*, *Ingeniero(a)*, and *Profesor(a)*. Also *Licenciado(a)*, which is the title for someone with a master's degree. These may be used in combination with *Señor*, *Señora*, or *Señorita* and with or without the individual's last name. For example, you may hear someone addressed as Doctor Pérez, Señor Doctor Pérez, or simply Señor Doctor. As a general rule, unmarried women are referred to as Señorita, not Señora.

Other Points of Protocol

Following the dictates of proper etiquette is a sign of good breeding. The general atmosphere between men and women, even in business, is more flirtatious than in the United States. It is important for women to accept that this is normal. It will do you no good to get defensive, and it might in fact do you some harm. This means that men should stand up when a woman enters the room, hold doors, and so on. Women have to be able to accept this courtesy gracefully, not begrudgingly.

Remember that business is a personal endeavor. A brusque, "businesslike" attitude will probably be interpreted as rudeness. Don't hurry into business discussions. Begin with some personal conversation and let things take their own course. Above all, don't be in a rush.

BUSINESS COMMUNICATION

The less than efficient mail service in most Central American countries is an unreliable conduit of business communication. The fax has all but replaced mail as the primary means of long-distance communication. If you must send hard copies, it's best to use a service such as FedEx to ensure delivery. E-mail, while gaining in popularity, is not as prevalent as it is in the United States. Avid e-mailers often find that their Central American colleagues check their e-mail less frequently than is the norm at home, slowing down the response time.

The telephone is of course an important tool for communication. However, if you are doing business from your home base abroad, you should remember that it is much more expensive for your Central American colleagues to make an international call than it is for you to call them. Especially if you are dealing with a smaller firm, you may find that it will facilitate communication if you take the initiative and call them. The most effective way to keep in touch is probably a combination of fax, phone, and e-mail. If you send a fax, call to let them know to expect it, and call again when it is time to follow up on the issue. E-mail can be used for less time-sensitive material, such as updates and status reports. Note, however, that e-mail is not available everywhere in Central America. Your colleagues in major metropolitan areas—and in major organizations—are likely to have an e-mail address, but it may not be available in outlying areas or in smaller organizations.

Don't expect your Central American business partners to have access to technology such as video conferencing, although some larger companies may have more advanced technology. They are also less likely to use voice mail or answering machines, so you will need to be prepared to call several times.

One of the most common complaints heard from anyone doing business with the United States from abroad is the complexity of the typical U.S. voice-mail system. The automated systems that require you to push a button for this and a button for that, followed by the pound key, an unfamiliar term to most non-Americans, are confusing, and have caused many a caller to hang up in despair rather than wade through the quagmire. If you would like to have your international customers, suppliers, or business partners contact you, you must make it easy for them. Simplify your voice-mail system as much as possible and explain how they can navigate your phone system to speak with someone in person; on many systems you can press 0 to be connected to an operator. Even better, make sure they have direct telephone numbers for key individuals or a point person for your team.

Although technology can enhance business, it is important to remember that face-to-face meetings are the most effective way to further your business in Central America. Easy enough if you are living there, but many people fail to make the effort to visit in person, considering it an inconvenience rather than a necessity. Many people have found that regular visits with their business partners have helped to ensure a prosperous business relationship. Don't rule out inviting someone to visit you in your home country either. The cost of such trips almost always pays for itself in terms of continued success.

WOMEN IN BUSINESS

While there are more and more women who work throughout Central America, few women are in high-level management positions. Women generally receive lower wages than men, and tend to be found in traditionally female occupations, such as secretaries, nurses, and teachers.

The role of women in society is evolving very slowly. The traditional role of a woman as wife and mother prevails over her professional role, and women are still largely responsible for child rearing, cooking, cleaning, and other domestic responsibilities. By the same token, the numbers of women entering traditionally male professions, such as medicine and law, are increasing. On the whole, however, working outside the home is largely viewed as a means of enhancing the family's income and not as a means of personal fulfillment.

Women in the Central American workplace take a different viewpoint from their American counterparts. Whereas American women want to be treated the same as their male colleagues, women in Central America maintain their femininity and gender roles in the workplace. They tend to be more soft-spoken and less aggressive, especially in the company of men, and are the recipients of the same courtesies from men as they are in social circumstances. Many foreign women find the more flirtatious atmosphere uncomfortable; it is important to learn to interpret things correctly and not read too much into flirtatious comments.

¡Adiós, Linda!

Women traveling in or moving to Central America will have to get used to *piropos*. These are the comments that perfect strangers offer to women to show their appreciation of their feminine form. The closest thing to this that most American women have experienced is the stereotypical loud whistle or catcall from the construction crew as they walk by, which most women consider degrading. Try not to make this association. Yes, you may hear an occasional vulgar comment. A *piropo*, however, is meant to please, not offend. It might be a simple ¡*Adiós, linda!* (Goodbye, beautiful!), something clever, such as "¡*Ay! ¡Si tu cocinas como caminas, quiero comer los rasgos!*" (Oh! If you cook like you walk, I want to eat the scraps) or even poetic, such as "*Quien fuera eterno para amarte toda la vida*" (Would that I were eternal to love you all my life).

The key to the *piropo* is the manner in which it is offered. It is not shouted at you from across the street, but quietly said to you alone, full of flirtation, but with subtlety, finesse, and respect. In point of fact, it is often uttered as you pass by, unaccompanied by ogling or even a backward glance from the man to see your response. When you hear a *piropo*, try to accept in light of the local culture. It is not necessary to respond to the *piropo*.

Strategies for Success

As an outsider, it is up to you to adapt to the local realities. It is important not to criticize openly what you may perceive to be inequality in the workplace or to take a stand for women's rights. Those types of actions will only cause resentment and can ultimately damage your ability to do business.

In some areas, managers may have experience working with American or Canadian businesswomen and may be aware of the expectations they have. However, you may have to contend with male colleagues who are unaccustomed to interacting with women as equals, and, if you are in a high-level position, with male subordinates who are uncomfortable with or even resentful of having a woman as their superior. It will take some effort to overcome any resistance. You may have to convince people of your expertise. In any case, it is important to maintain a sense of dignity and poise.

A woman in a leadership position, such as someone leading a negotiating team, should make it clear from the outset that she is in charge. This is not necessarily accomplished with a brash statement. Rather, it should become evident by the respect that her team members show her by referring decisions to her, and by more subtle means, such as proper introductions and having her name at the top of the list of team members.

While you are in Central America you will need to take care to avoid any suggestion of impropriety. For example, one expatriate manager in Panama City found that her social life was under as much scrutiny as her actions as a manager. She soon learned that women in Central America do not go to a bar alone to have a drink after work, and that if they do, they are fair game for any man in the place, since it's assumed that they are looking for male company. There is simply a different set of rules for women. Luckily, someone warned her early on that a woman's conduct in her personal life would reflect on her professional life, so she managed to avoid any serious problems. It did, however, make for many lonely nights until she was able to establish a social network. Unfortunately, many people view single American women as promiscuous simply because they are unmarried or unaccompanied by a spouse. You will probably find that your actions are under more scrutiny than those of your male counterparts.

If you do find yourself the subject of unwanted attention by male business colleagues, it can be difficult to extract yourself from the situation without wounding the man's ego and damaging the business transaction in the process. A calm, good-humored reaction is preferable to indignity or outrage. In extreme cases, you may have to let the man know that you do not welcome his advances and that he must stop.

It is altogether easier to maintain a professional relationship if you avoid situations where you are alone with a male colleague. If you would like to have a business dinner, invite another person to go along, and go to a restaurant suited to a business dinner, not a romantic tête-à-tête. If possible, include your colleague's spouse to avoid any potential for jealousy.

A final note for business women: If you invite a man to lunch or dinner for business purposes, you will find that he will probably not allow you to pay for the meal. If you want for the meal to be on you, your best bet is to either arrange payment for the meal beforehand or excuse yourself after the meal and take care of the bill before it arrives at the table.

SEVEN

BUSINESS STEP-BY-STEP

THE PERSONAL TOUCH

Personal relationships are an important part of business throughout Central America. They are the key to getting information and for making the contacts you need to succeed. Businesspeople in Central America spend a considerable amount of time getting to know a potential business partner, often over coffee or a meal. Your character carries as much weight as your expertise. Once you have established a foundation of mutual trust, it is important to continue to nurture the relationship, for this is the oil that keeps the machinery of business running smoothly.

It is often difficult for Americans to understand the need to develop personal relationships in Central America. It is a mistake to try to enter into a Central American business environment with your eye only on the goal. Or rather, you must alter your perspective of what the goal is. You are likely to discover that to your Central American business partner or colleagues, the personal relationships that they enjoy with one another are as much a part of the goal as the business that is generated. You must therefore enter the Central American market—as a business partner or as a manager—with the intention of investing your time as well as your money.

Making Contact

If you are new to doing business in Central America or with a particular company, it can be beneficial to arrange a third-party introduction. A mutual acquaintance can help pave the way by establishing your credibility. Look for potential contacts within your current business network. This could be a client, a supplier, or a service provider such as your lawyer or accountant.

If you are unable to find an appropriate contact, don't give up on the idea of doing business in Central America. While a third party is helpful, it is not by any means mandatory. If you are looking for potential business partners, consider using one of the many business resources available through chambers of commerce and other offices that facilitate trade with Central America.

Once you have located a potential business partner, it is important to find the appropriate person to approach. An introductory fax, explaining your proposal, followed by a telephone call will help you determine if there is any potential for the partnership. However, you should be prepared to make a trip down to Central America to discuss the idea in detail.

Getting Down to Business

An offshoot of the topic of relationship building is the importance of social conversation in business. As mentioned above, trust and character are important measures in the decision to do business with an individual, or even a company, as represented by that individual. This is accomplished, naturally, though conversation, not about business, but about the things that make us who we are.

An American whose typical approach to a business meeting is "Hi, how are you? Lovely weather we're having today, now about your order..." will find himself regarded with suspicion, and the order he is talking about may quietly evaporate. Even an amount of "small talk" that an American would consider excessive would probably not even begin to satisfy someone from Central America. After all, if you don't know each other well; is it not important to move slowly to allow each other time to feel comfortable? And if you do know each other, isn't it important to take every opportunity to catch up with each other and strengthen the friendship?

The best advice is to exercise patience. Remember, what you consider "small" talk is not small to them.

MEETINGS AND APPOINTMENTS

Perhaps the best time to schedule a meeting in Central America is between mid-morning and early afternoon. As you are planning, keep in mind that most businesspeople take extended lunch hours; most work until later in the evening to compensate for their siestas. If you're scheduling a lunch meeting, you are unlikely to get many people around the table at noon, since lunch is usually taken around 2:00 P.M. Likewise, if you're planning a business dinner, remember that people tend to eat dinner late.

When you make an appointment in Central America, you can assume that it will be written in pencil, not in pen. In other words, something may supercede the meeting, or you may be kept waiting for some time. While this can be a power play—a demonstration that someone has the ability to make you wait—it is more often than not the result of differing views of time. As has been mentioned several times, the Central American view of time is more flexible than that of most Americans, so don't take it personally. This doesn't mean, however, that it is acceptable for you to waltz into a meeting or show up at an appointment 30 minutes late. You should be on time, and if you are unavoidably delayed, try to call ahead.

Meetings, in a way, are an extension of the relationship-building process. They tend to begin with more social conversation before moving on to the business at hand. Meetings in Central America tend to be rather chaotic by American standards. Central Americans are not as keen as Americans on setting an agenda in the first place, much less adhering to it religiously. While they may amicably agree to an agenda, the group is not likely to stick to it. It is common to find that some meeting participants will be late, some will come in and out of the meeting, and there will be interruptions. Americans who like an orderly meeting where topics are addressed in order with everyone's full attention will find their blood pressure rising. This is not to say that meetings are unproductive in Central America. They simply have a different approach to them.

NEGOTIATING

Preparing

If you will be involved in formal negotiations, you will want to do some homework first. It's a good idea to provide the other team with a list of who will be attending, including a description of each person's level of responsibility and role on the negotiating team. Request a similar list from the other team to ensure that the appropriate people are included on each team. The best approach is to be sure that your teams are matched in terms of the status and titles of the team members.

You should also determine the level of authority of members of the other team. Find out who will be leading the team and determine if he will have the power to make the final decision. If the leader is not the decision-maker, factor that into your strategy in terms of the timeline and approach.

Strategy

Negotiating is akin to a game wherein both partners are expected to engage in give-and-take bargaining, with the result being a win-win situation. The meeting will begin with several minutes of social conversation. As has been stressed throughout the book, you should not underestimate the importance of this time, since it is a significant part of building relationships and trust. The most successful mindset is one that considers this a part of the negotiation, not merely a nuisance that must be endured before business can be discussed.

The negotiation opens with a formal welcome from the leader of the host team, followed by the leader of the guest team. At this point the agenda and structure of the meetings can be reviewed and clarified as necessary.

The Central American team will probably show deference to the team leader, who is the main spokesperson for the team. Individual team members will be involved in discussions in their area of technical expertise.

An experienced negotiator may use a variety of tactics, such as pressuring for concessions based on friendship, using a display of temper, or using the opposing team's deadlines against them.

Common Pitfalls

Negotiations over the years have failed for many reasons, including the following:

Deadlines. This can be exploited by a negotiator who is comfortable with a more relaxed perspective on time. The best way to circumvent this is to be generous in scheduling the time it will take to complete the negotiation. Be prepared to extend your visit or return at a later date if necessary. Don't put deadlines on yourself that can be used against you.

Impatience. Someone who rushes through the business of getting to know one another in order to discuss the details of a deal is considered rude and untrustworthy. Because decisions are made at least in part based on a subjective evaluation of you as a person, refusing to take the time or rushing through the social aspects of a negotiation can scuttle the whole deal.

Unwillingness to "play the game." View the negotiation as a card game, where one card is revealed at a time. Putting all your cards on the table at once with a take-it-or-leave-it attitude is arrogant and is unlikely to be an effective tactic. Remember, however, that the game must result with both sides winning.

Failure to build personal relationships. Your personal character and the trust that you are able to build with your counterparts are key ingredients of a solid business relationship. If trust breaks down, so will the negotiations.

Rotating team members. This is closely linked to the point above. If the members of your team change, personal relationships must be rebuilt. Don't assume that one team member can just pick up where another one left off. Too much turnover sends the signal that your company is unstable or that it does not consider that particular deal to be important.

Pressing the legal issues. Again, this relates to trust. If you conclude the negotiation by shaking hands while holding out the contract to be signed, you are implying that there is a lack of trust on your part. This does not mean that all legal formalities, such as a contract, should be ignored. On the contrary, they are very important; they just need to be handled in a sensitive manner. If necessary, you can reassure your counterparts that while you have no doubts, the documentation is a formality required by the company's lawyers.

Breaking off negotiations on a sour note. If the negotiation is not working out, the worst thing you can do is part company with bad feelings. Keep in mind that the way you conduct your business with one person can have a impact on other business, direct or indirect, due to the extensive network of personal contacts that come into play in Central America. For instance, you might burn a bridge with an executive in one company, only to find out that he is friends with someone in another company you do business with; that relationship can become poisoned as a byproduct. Like a pebble tossed into a pond, your actions can have rippling consequences.

MANAGING

The task of managing in another culture can be quite daunting. In order to be successful, it's important to understand the norms of your host culture and decide how your own management style will mesh with those norms. The most successful managers are those who maintain a flexible approach and are open to incorporating aspects of the local management style into their own.

The typical management style in Central America, consistent with the hierarchical structure, is fairly authoritarian and patriarchal. The role is in essence that of an authoritarian, autocratic father figure. Many small and medium-size companies are family owned or began as family operations. There is great respect for authority, and that authority is at the highest levels of the company. Even in larger corporations, the power rests with a few people at the very top. Decisions are made by those at the top and are followed without question or discussion by those below.

The typical hierarchical structure does not leave much room for delegation of authority. Delegation in the Central American context tends to mean delegation of certain tasks and not necessarily of responsibility for any business area. If responsibility is given to an individual, he is often not empowered with the authority and decision-making power to support his responsibilities. The side effect of this situation is typically an accompanying lack of accountability. One of the frustrating problems encountered by outsiders trying to do business in Central America is locating the individual ostensibly in charge of an aspect of business, only to find out that he is unable to make a decision without the approval of his superiors. This means that everything from making a sale to getting a specific piece of information can take a considerable amount of time.

This is slowly changing in some countries, such as Mexico, as a new generation of managers, many of whom attended a university abroad, advocate a different approach to business, including delegation of responsibility, as well as the authority and accountability that go along with it. However, it is a slow evolution and the traditional way of doing things continues to dominate.

Loyalty

Traditionally, workers were motivated by loyalty to the boss or patron, often the owner of the company. The employer/employee relationship was quasi-familial in nature, since the worker relied on his employer to ensure his welfare, from food and clothing to medical care and even housing. The boss was even someone to turn to with personal problems. In this environment, a worker hired was part of the company family for life.

In today's economy, however, most workers must rely on themselves, not their company. This has meant a decrease in loyalty to the company and an increase in turnover as people look for jobs with higher salaries. The organizations that experience the lowest turnover have been those that have retained a focus on their employees. An agreeable work atmosphere and policies that take into consideration personal needs and priorities remain important to the average employee. A corporate culture that focuses solely on the bottom line is less likely to attract and keep employees.

When compared to the United States, however, there is still a greater bond between the company and the employee. The company has a certain obligation to provide for its employees, including avoiding layoffs. Most employees are quite proud to be a part of the company they work for.

Personal loyalty to one's boss continues to play an important part in business. This loyalty, of course, must be earned by establishing a relationship built on mutual respect and trust.

Competition and Conflict

The Central American mindset tends to prefer a friendly atmosphere free of conflict. Competition with one's colleagues, which includes elements of conflict and confrontation, is not looked upon favorably. The idea of ruthlessly fighting one's way to the top is repugnant to most Central American managers.

Maintaining personal dignity is also very important. Tact and diplomacy are preferable to expressing oneself bluntly, especially if such an approach would wound the dignity of the other person.

These issues have many implications for managers. It has a direct impact on the superior/subordinate relationship. Subordinates are reluctant to question their supervisors. A manager who holds a meeting for the purpose of discussing an idea or proposal may find that his employees are hesitant to make any comments that would imply criticism of the manager or argue with their colleagues.

In the same vein, a supervisor who needs to take corrective action with a subordinate must be careful not to call that person on the carpet in public. A large measure of diplomacy is also called for in these instances. In the United States, the general rule is that emotion has no place in business. People are expected to be able to accept "constructive criticism" without taking it personally, allowing the person to develop professionally. No such rule exists in the Central American environment, and an outright statement of criticism, even if it is meant to help, is taken personally.

HIRING AND PROMOTION

In Central America, most companies began as—and many still are—family-owned businesses. Trust and loyalty are characteristics valued in an employee, and it is generally considered difficult to find those qualities in people outside of one's family and close friends. In addition, the family takes priority in most people's lives. This combination of values and circumstances inevitably leads to a nepotistic environment, which is often discomfiting to Americans, who feel that everyone should be hired and promoted according to ability.

Most Central Americans prefer to hire from the inside. That is, to hire a family member or friend, or at the very least, someone who comes highly recommended from a trusted third party. However, the reality of business today does not always allow this luxury, and more and more companies are turning to advertising and placement agencies to fill positions as they grow. An expatriate manager, however, still needs to be attuned to the norms of the company if he or she is in a position to hire staff. For example, if the second in command recommends that you hire his nephew for a position, you will need to consider carefully the potential result of a refusal on your relationship with that person. Remember that relationships are the cornerstone of doing business in Central America and impact every aspect of business.

Advancement

Most people in the upper echelons of business in Central America are there not because of what they know, but who they know. Although ability plays a role in professional advancement, personal contacts are even more important. The savvy young manager realizes that getting to the top is as much a matter of politics and influence as much as it is ability. Supervisors tend to promote the people who have shown devotion and a cooperative attitude.

As is the case with other ideas, this particular business practice is changing somewhat in larger organizations. These companies are placing more emphasis on qualifications and achievement as criteria for advancement.

Opportunities for advancement in smaller companies are often quite limited, especially if the company is family owned. In those companies, the top jobs are passed to family members; non-family employees often must leave the company or start their own business in order to move up the chain.

PRESENTING YOUR IDEAS
AND MAKING SPEECHES

An American who arrives at a Central American office, turns on the overhead projector, states the facts, and wraps it up is not going to win kudos for his professionalism. Instead, his Central American colleagues are likely to be baffled, if not offended, by his abruptness. Americans value succinctness and like to get to the bottom line. Central Americans like to have more background information given to them. In addition, the American style of presenting is essentially a statement of the facts, and the audience is expected to make a decision based solely on the facts. Central Americans tend to focus more on the style of the presentation, and the appeal to the audience is likely to include an emotional aspect.

Speeches follow this pattern as well. Americans have an acronym to follow when making a speech: KISS, or Keep It Short and Simple. In keeping with their value of time, an American audience views sitting through a long-winded speech as an ordeal. Central Americans, by contrast, tend to give lengthy speeches filled with flowery language, emotional appeals, and great enthusiasm.

BUSINESS ENTERTAINING

Socializing is an important part of business in Central America. It can take many forms, such as lunch, dinner, or just a cup of coffee. Most negotiations, business conferences, and business visits include one or more social events, often dinner and an evening of entertainment. It is important that you attend these events and remember that they are social occasions meant to celebrate your friendship, not an extension of the business meeting.

Spouses are not usually included in business-related events, such as a dinner in the first week of a negotiation. However, they are often included in other, more social, events. Once you have established yourself with a business partner and you return to the country for a visit, you will probably have occasion to go to dinner with your host and his spouse.

Being invited to someone's home is an indication that your relationship has progressed to a friendship. Treat it as the honor it is, and accept the invitation if at all possible; repeatedly declining to visit someone's home can have a detrimental effect on the relationship. Welcome it as an opportunity to take your relationship with your colleague to an even higher level of friendship and intimacy.

GIFT GIVING

Gift giving can be tricky business in another culture for many reasons. Not only do you have to take into consideration the traditions of the country, you need to be aware of any potential repercussions for yourself and your company if you give an inappropriate business gift. You will want to familiarize yourself with your company's policy regarding the giving of gifts; many companies put a dollar limit on gifts.

That said, it is common to give gifts in Mexico and Central America. It is part of the relationship-building process. You should, however, wait until you have established an amiable relationship; if you go down on your initial trip and shower people you have never met with gifts, it is more likely to be construed as a bribe than as a gesture of friendship. By the same token, the actual giving of the gift should follow business, not lead up to it. Wait until the negotiations have been completed or until your business meeting is over and the atmosphere has become more informal and social.

Gifts should be given some thought, not just picked up at the last minute at the duty-free shop at the airport before you board your plane. Selecting a gift that suits your colleague's personality or interests is a gesture of genuine concern and interest in that person. Giving a bottle of wine to a colleague who on your last trip down took you to a restaurant just so you could try their excellent brandy is less than thoughtful; bringing him an excellent bottle from your own cellar tells him that you were not only paying attention, you were actually thinking about him as you selected the gift.

You will need to be careful about giving a gift to a colleague of the opposite gender, since you do not want your innocent gift to be misconstrued as some sort of personal advance. Men can present the gift with the disclaimer that it was sent by his wife (or another female; perhaps a female business colleague who is not present) to prevent any appearance of impropriety. Women can turn that scenario around by offering the gift on behalf of her and her husband, a boss, a colleague, or the team as appropriate.

It is a nice gesture to bring a gift for the secretary of an important person. Appropriate gifts might be perfume, a scarf, or a small piece of gold jewelry. Giving a token gift to a secretary in the public sector who performs a service for you will keep you in her good graces, which can come in handy the next time you need a favor. Other suggestions for business gifts are gold pens, desk clocks, calculators, Scotch, or cognac.

A NOTE ON USING INTERPRETERS

You may find that many of your Central American colleagues speak English, depending on which country you are in. However, English is less prevalent in some areas, and you may well find yourself in a circumstance where an interpreter is necessary or desirable.

An interpreter can be a terrific resource for more than just language. An interpreter who is either bi-cultural or is knowledgeable about the cultural differences between your country and the country you are visiting can provide you not only with linguistic services but also with invaluable information about protocol, the nuances of the local business culture, and the interpretation of not only words but non-verbal cues and hidden meanings.

While it may seem easier to let your hosts provide an interpreter—after all, it will be one less thing on a very long list to worry about—you should carefully consider the possible impact of that option. Absolutely objective interpreters are hard to come by; the interpreter's loyalty is most likely going to be toward his or her employer. Selecting your own interpreter ensures that your interests will be looked after. Even if your hosts are providing interpretive services, bringing your own interpreter will help verify the content of the exchange.

- Whenever possible, use an interpreter who is familiar with your industry and even with your company. If your company does not have access to a suitable individual and must hire someone unfamiliar to you or your company, arrange to meet with the interpreter before the meetings in order to brief him on your company, your goals, and your expectations. Provide the interpreter with as much documentation as possible to allow him to prepare for the meeting.

- If you happen to have a Spanish-speaking team member and are relying on that person to interpret for the team, don't also expect him or her to enter into the negotiations. It not only becomes confusing, it is virtually impossible, because interpreting requires a great deal of focus and concentration. So even though a key member of your team speaks Spanish, it is still wise to have an official interpreter who is not part of the actual negotiation.

- If each team has an interpreter present, each will translate the comments of his or her respective team. If only one is present, he will obviously be responsible for all translation.

- Always address the person to whom the comment or question is directed, not the interpreter. This takes practice, as most people tend to automatically turn to face the interpreter.

- Don't overwhelm the interpreter with words. You should pause for interpretation after every two or three sentences.

- Try to keep your sentences as uncomplicated as possible. A long, rambling sentence is very difficult to translate.

- Keep your vocabulary as simple as the situation will allow. You should also take the time to ensure that the interpreter has a vocabulary compatible with your needs, and go over any technical details with him or her.

- Avoid slang and colloquialisms. They may not be understood or, potentially even more disastrous, misunderstood if they are interpreted literally.
- The interpreter is not a machine. Interpreting takes an enormous amount of mental energy and is very draining. Allow at least a brief rest period after every hour or so. This is another argument in favor of having separate interpreters.
- If you are having trouble making yourself understood—and this goes for direct communication as well as interpreter-assisted communication—do not under any circumstance repeat your question or comment in ever-increasing volumes. The problem is comprehension, not hearing. Rephrase the statement until you reach understanding.

EIGHT

LAST NOTES

We hope that this book has given you some insight into Central America and prepared you for a successful, rewarding stay in Central America. The practical tips contained in this book should help you feel more comfortable as your journey begins, and the information on Central American culture will help you navigate as your journey continues. Finally, you'll find that the language section contains the most essential words and phrases; remember that even a little Spanish will make a world of difference.

In addition to the specific information covered in this book, don't forget these important guidelines for cross-cultural interaction anywhere around the globe:

- Learn about the culture you are visiting. The better you understand its culture the more prepared you will be to tune your skills to its frequency.
- Keep your sense of humor. Things are guaranteed to go wrong now and again, and you will make mistakes. Your best defense is your ability to find humor in the situation.
- And finally, respect other cultures. Just because it's not the way you do things doesn't mean it's wrong.

¡Buena Suerte! in the exciting new environment that awaits you in Central America.

NINE

LANGUAGE NOTES

SPANISH ALPHABET AND PRONUNCIATION

Letter	Name	Letter	Name	Letter	Name
a	ah	j	HOH-tah	r	EH-reh
b	beh	k	kah	s	Eh-seh
c	seh	l	EH-leh	t	teh
d	deh	m	EH-meh	u	oo
e	eh	n	EH-neh	v	veh
f	EH-feh	ñ	EH-nyeh	w	doh-bleh-VEH
g	heh	o	oh	x	EH-kees
h	AH-cheh	p	peh	y	ee-gree-EH-gah
i	ee	q	koo	z	SEH-tah

VOWELS

SPANISH SOUND	APPROXIMATE SOUND IN ENGLISH	EXAMPLE
a	(father)	trabajar (to work)
e	(ace, but cut off sharply)	señor (mister)
i	(fee)	día (day)
o	(note)	pistola (pistol)
u	(rule)	mucho (much)
y	(feet)	y (and) [only a vowel when standing alone]

DIPTHONGS

SPANISH SOUND	APPROXIMATE SOUND IN ENGLISH	EXAMPLE
ai/ay	(aisle)	bailar, hay
au	(now)	auto
ei	(may)	peine
ia	(yarn)	gracias
io	(yodel)	adiós
iu	(you)	ciudad
oi/oy	(oy)	oigo
		estoy
ua	(wand)	cuando
ue	(wet)	bueno
ui/uy	(Louis)	cuidado
		muy

CONSONANTS

The letters *k* and *w* appear in Spanish in foreign words like *kilowatt*, *kilometer*. In some countries, the *k* is spelled with the Spanish equivalent, *qu*: *quilómetro*. The *w* in Spanish sounds like an English *v*: *kilowatt*.

SPANISH SOUND	APPROXIMATE SOUND IN ENGLISH	EXAMPLE
l/m/n/p/s/t	similar to corresponding English consonants	
b	b (boy), at the beginning of a word or after a consonant.	bueno, mambo
	like v (vain) but softer, allowing air to pass between lips.	cabeza
c (before e/i)	s (certain)	cena
c (before a/o/u)	k (catch)	como
cc	(tax)	lección
ch	ch (church)	mucho
d	like th (the) but softer, allowing air to pass between the lips.	verdad
g (before i/e)	h (he)	gente
g (before a/o/u)	g (go)	ganar
h	always silent	hasta
j	hard h (he)	jefe
ll	y (yet) in Latin America lli (million) in Spain	pollo
ñ	ny (canyon)	caña
qu	k (kite)	que
r	r (throw), but trilled	pero

r	r rolled, double trill	rosa
rr	r rolled, double trill	carro
v	v (vote), but softer, allowing air to pass between lips.	viernes
x	x (tax)	taxi
y	y (yet)	yo
z	(say)	zona

THE SPANISH LANGUAGE

Word Order

The basic word order of Spanish is the same as in English: subject-verb-object.

El mesero trae la pizza.　　The waiter brings the pizza.
　S　　V　　O　　　　　　　S　　V　　　O

Nouns and Adjectives

All nouns in Spanish have gender. *El* (the) and *un* (a/an) are used with masculine nouns, and *la* and *una* are used with feminine nouns. To form the plural, simply add an *–s* or *–es* to the singular noun. *Los* is the article used with plural masculine nouns, and *las* is used with plural feminine nouns. Adjectives in Spanish change to agree with the nouns they modify. Adjective endings follow the same pattern as with nouns: *el niño curioso* (the curious boy); *la niña curiosa* (the curious girl); *los niños curiosos* (the curious boys); and *las niñas curiosas* (the curious girls). Notice that most adjectives in Spanish come after the nouns they modify.

Verbs

Spanish verbs undergo various changes to indicate subject, tense, or mood. *El mesero lleva la pizza.* (The waiter brings the pizza.) *Llevamos una botella.* (We bring a bottle.) *Llevaban unas flores.* (They were bringing some flowers.) *Llevaría el queso.* (I would bring the cheese.) *El Señor Martínez llevará el dinero.* (Mr. Martínez will bring the money.)

Phrases

You don't need to master the entire Spanish language to spend a week in Latin America, but taking charge of a few key phrases in the language can aid you in just getting by. The following supplement will allow you to get a hotel room, get around town, order a drink at the end of the day, and get help in case of an emergency.

Listen to the phrase and repeat what you hear in the space provided.

COMMON GREETINGS

Hello/Good morning.	Hola/Buenas días.
Good evening.	Buenas tardes.
Good-bye.	Adiós/Hasta luego.
Title for a married woman or an older unmarried woman	Señora
Title for a young and unmarried woman	Señorita
Title for a man	Señor
How are you? (informal)	¿Cómo estás?
Fine, thanks. And you? (informal)	Bien, gracias, y tu?
How are you? (formal)	¿Cómo está?
Fine, thanks. And you? (formal)	Bien, gracias, y usted?
What is your name?	¿Cómo se llama?
My name is . . .	Mi nombre es...
Nice to meet you.	Un placer conocerle.
I'll see you later.	Nos vemos más tarde.

POLITE EXPRESSIONS

Please	Por favor
Thank you.	Gracias.
Thank you very much.	Muchas gracias.
You're welcome.	De nada.
Yes, thank you.	Sí, gracias.
No, thank you.	No, gracias.
I beg your pardon?	Perdón, me lo podría repetir.
I'm sorry.	Lo siento.
Pardon me. (informal)	Perdón.
Pardon me. (formal)	Disculpe.
That's okay.	Está bien.
It doesn't matter.	No importa.
Do you speak English?	¿Habla usted inglés?
Yes.	Sí.
No.	No.
Maybe.	Tal vez.
I can speak a little.	Hablo un poco.
I understand a little.	Entiendo un poco.
I don't understand.	No entiendo.
I don't speak Spanish very well.	No hablo español muy bien.
Would you repeat that, please?	Puede repetir lo que dijo, por favor.
I don't know.	No lo sé.
No problem.	No hay problema.
It's my pleasure.	Es un placer.

NEEDS AND QUESTION WORDS

I'd like ...	Yo quisiera...
I need ...	Necesito...
What would you like?	¿Qué le gustaría?
Please bring me...	Por favor, traígame...
I'm looking for...	Estoy buscando...
I'm hungry.	Tengo hambre.
I'm thirsty.	Tengo sed.

It's important.	Es importante.
It's urgent.	Es urgente.
How?	¿Cómo?
How much?	¿Cuánto cuesta?
How many?	¿Cuántos?
Which?	¿Cuál?
What?	¿Qué?
What kind of?	¿Qué clase de?
Who?	¿Quién?
Where?	¿Dónde?
When?	¿Cuándo?
What does this mean?	¿Qué significa esto?
What does that mean?	¿Qué significa eso?
How do you say . . . in Spanish?	¿Cómo se dice . . . en español?

AT THE AIRPORT

Where is . . .	¿Dónde está...
customs?	la aduana?
passport control?	el control de pasaportes?
the information booth?	el módulo de información?
the ticketing counter?	el mostrador de boletos?
the baggage claim?	el reclamo de equipaje?
the ground transportation?	el transporte terrestre?
Is there a bus service to the city?	¿Existe servicio de autobús a la ciudad?
Where are . . .	¿Dónde están...
the international departures?	las salidas internacionales?
the international arrivals?	las llegadas internacionales?
What is your nationality?	¿Cuál es tu nacionalidad?
I am an American.	Soy estadounidense/ americano.
I am Canadian.	Soy canadiense.

AT THE HOTEL, RESERVING A ROOM

I would like a room.	Quiero un cuarto/una habitación.
for one person	para una persona
for two people	para dos personas
for tonight	por una noche
for two nights	por dos noches
for a week	por una semana
Do you have a different room?	¿Tiene una habitación diferente?
with a bath	con baño
with a shower	con regadera
with a toilet	con escusado
with air-conditioning	con aire acondicionado
How much is it?	¿Cuánto cuesta?
My bill, please.	La cuenta, por favor.

AT THE RESTAURANT

Where can we find a good restaurant?	¿Dónde podemos encontrar un buen restaurante?
We'd like a(n) ... restaurant.	Nos gustaría un restaurante...
casual	informal.
elegant	formal.
fast-food	de comida rápida.
inexpensive	barato.
seafood	de mariscos.
vegetarian	vegetariano.
Café	Café
A table for two	Una mesa para dos
Waiter, a menu please.	Mesero, el menú por favor.
The wine list, please.	La carta de vinos, por favor.
Appetizers	Aperitivos
Main course	Plato principal
Dessert	Postre
What would you like?	¿Qué le gustaría?
What would you like to drink?	¿Qué le gustaría tomar?

Can you recommend a good wine?	Puede recomendar un buen vino?
Wine, please.	Vino, por favor.
Beer, please.	Cerveza, por favor.
I didn't order this.	Yo no ordené esto.
That's all, thanks.	Eso es todo, gracias.
The check, please.	La cuenta, por favor.
Cheers! To your health!	¡Salud! ¡A su salud!

OUT ON THE TOWN

Where can I find ...	¿Dónde puedo encontrar...
an art museum?	un museo de arte?
a museum of natural history?	un museo de historia natural?
a history museum?	un museo de historia?
a gallery?	una galería?
interesting architecture?	arquitectura interesante?
a church?	una iglesia?
the zoo?	un zoológico?
I'd like ...	Quisiera...
to see a play.	ver una obra de teatro.
to see a movie.	ver una película.
to go to a concert.	ir a un concierto.
to go to opera.	ir a la ópera.
to go sightseeing.	hacer un recorrido.
to go on a bike ride.	ir a un paseo en bicicleta.

SHOPPING

Where is the best place to go shopping for ...	¿Cuál es el mejor lugar para comprar...
clothes?	ropa?
food?	comida?
souvenirs?	recuerdos?
furniture?	muebles?

fabric?	tela?
antiques?	antigüedades?
books?	libros?
sporting goods?	artículos deportivos?
electronics?	artículos electrónicos?
computers?	computadoras?

DIRECTIONS

Excuse me. Where is . . .	Disculpe. ¿Dónde está...
the bus stop?	la parada del autobús?
the subway station?	la estación del metro?
the rest room?	el baño?
the taxi stand?	el sitio de taxis?
the nearest bank?	el banco más cercano?
the hotel?	el hotel?
To the right	A la derecha
To the left	A la izquierda
Straight ahead	De frente
It's near here.	Está cerca de aqui.
Go back.	Regrese.
Next to . . .	Junto a...

NUMBERS

Cardinal

0	cero	10	diez
1	uno	11	once
2	dos	12	doce
3	tres	13	trece
4	cuatro	14	catorce
5	cinco	15	quince
6	seis	16	dieciseis
7	siete	17	diecisiete
8	ocho	18	dieciocho
9	nueve	19	diecinueve

20	veinte	80	ochenta
21	veintiuno	90	noventa
22	veintidos	100	cien
23	veintitres	1,000	mil
30	treinta	1,100	mil cien
40	cuarenta	2,000	dos mil
50	cincuenta	10,000	diez mil
60	sesenta	100,000	cien mil
70	setenta	1,000,000	un millón

Ordinal

first	primero	seventeenth	décimo séptimo
second	segundo	eighteenth	décimo octavo
third	tercero	nineteenth	décimo noveno
fourth	cuarto	twentieth	vigésimo
fifth	quinto	twenty-first	vigésimo primero
sixth	sexto	twenty-second	vigésimo segundo
seventh	séptimo	thirtieth	trigésimo
eighth	octavo	fortieth	cuadragésimo
ninth	noveno	fiftieth	quincuagésimo
tenth	décimo	sixtieth	sexagésimo
eleventh	décimo primero	seventieth	heptagésimo
twelfth	décimo segundo	eightieth	octagésimo
thirteenth	décimo tercero	ninetieth	nonagésimo
fourteenth	décimo cuarto	hundredth	centésimo
fifteenth	décimo quinto	thousandth	milésimo
sixteenth	décimo sexto		

TIME

What time is it?	¿Qué hora es?
It is noon.	Mediodía.

It is midnight.	Medianoche.
It is 9:00 A.M.	Son las nueve de la mañana.
It is 1:00 P.M.	Es la una de la tarde.
It is 3 o'clock.	Son las tres en punto.
It is 5:15.	Son las cinco y cuarto.
It is 7:30.	Son las siete y media.
It is 9:45.	Son cuarto para las diez.
Now	Ahora
Later	Después
Immediately	Ahora
Soon	Pronto

DAYS OF THE WEEK / MONTHS OF THE YEAR

Monday	lunes
Tuesday	martes
Wednesday	miércoles
Thursday	jueves
Friday	viernes
Saturday	sábado
Sunday	domingo
What day is today?	¿Qué día es hoy?
January	enero
February	febrero
March	marzo
April	abril
May	mayo
June	junio
July	julio
August	agosto
September	septiembre
October	octubre
November	noviembre
December	diciembre

What is the date today?	¿Qué día es hoy?
Today is Thursday, September 22.	Hoy es jueves, veintidos de septiembre.
Yesterday was Wednesday, September 21.	Ayer fue miércoles, veintiuno de septiembre.
Tomorrow is Friday, September 23.	Mañana es viernes, veintitres de septiembre.

MODERN CONNECTIONS

Where can I find ...	¿Dónde puedo encontrar...
a telephone?	un teléfono?
a fax machine?	un fax?
an Internet connection?	una conexión de internet?
How do I call the United States?	Cómo llamo a los Estados Unidos?

I need ...	Necesito...
a fax sent.	enviar un fax.
a hook-up to the Internet.	conectarme a internet.
a computer.	una computadora.
a package sent overnight.	enviar un paquete por mensajeria.
some copies made.	hacer unas copias.
a VCR and monitor.	una videocasetera y un monitor.
an overhead projector and markers.	un proyector y unos marcadores.

EMERGENCIES AND SAFETY

Help!	¡Ayuda!
Fire!	¡Fuego!
I need a doctor.	Necesito un doctor.
Call an ambulance!	¡Llamen a una ambulancia!

What happened?	¿Qué sucedió?
I am/My wife is/My husband is/ My friend is/Someone is ...	Yo estoy/Mi esposa está/ Mi esposo está/Mi amigo(a) está/Alguien está...
I am/someone is very sick.	Yo estoy/Alguien está muy enfermo.
I am/someone is having a heart attack.	Yo estoy/Alguien está sufriendo un infarto (ataque al corazón).
I am/someone is choking.	Yo me estoy/Alguien se está ahogando.
I am/someone is losing consciousness.	Yo estoy/Alguien está perdiendo el conocimiento.
I am/someone is about to vomit.	Yo estoy/Alguien está por vomitar.
I am/someone is having a seizure.	Yo estoy/Alguien está sufriendo un ataque.
I am/someone is stuck.	Yo estoy/Alguien está atorado(a).

I can't breathe.	No puedo respirar.
I tripped and fell.	Me tropeze y caí.
I cut myself.	Me corte.
I drank too much.	Bebí demasiado.
I don't know.	No lo sé.

I've injured my ...	Me lastimé...
head.	la cabeza.
neck.	el cuello.
back.	la espalda.
arm.	el brazo.
leg.	la pierna.
foot.	el pie.
eye(s).	el ojo/los ojos.

I've been robbed.	Me robaron.

Passports. Be sure that each member of your family has one, and that each is valid for the length of your assignment. Children should have separate passports; otherwise they will not be allowed to travel alone or with an adult other than their parents, even in an emergency.

Visas. Check with the embassy of any countries you will be in for necessary visas. Requirements vary by country, especially for international relocation. As you travel, don't overlook the fact that some countries require a transit visa for people passing through the country, even if you don't get off your plane or train.

Vaccinations/inoculations. Check for recommended vaccinations or inoculations for the country you will be living in, as well as any countries you intend to visit. (This is listed on the U.S. Department of State Consular Information Sheet; see Copy of Important Documents.) The Department of Health and Human Services' Office of Public Health Services is able to issue an International Certificate of Vaccination containing your personal history of vaccinations. The ICV is approved by the World Health Organization.

Insurance. Make sure that your insurance will cover you while you are abroad. Check now, before you need it. If it won't, do some research to find out how to supplement or change your insurance so that you are adequately covered.

International driver's permits. Although you can use your U.S. or Canadian driver's license in some countries, it is generally advisable to obtain an international driver's permit. This is available from the AAA for a small fee and does not require taking a test. International driver's permits are valid for one year; after that time, you may have to get a local driver's license. Be sure that you get a permit that is valid for the country(ies) that you will be driving in.

Pets. Check with the consulate of your host country to find out about restrictions and requirements for bringing pets into the country. Most countries require a health and immunization certificate from a veterinarian; some have quarantine periods upon arrival.

Medical records. Obtain complete medical records for each member of your family. Have one copy on hand for the trip in case of an emergency.

Prescriptions and medication. If you or anyone in your family takes prescription medication, especially one containing narcotics, have your doctor give you a letter stating what the drug is and why it is necessary. Be sure you get a list of the Latin names of all prescription drugs from your doctor, since brand names vary from country to country. Take a six-month supply of any prescription medication, if possible. All medication, prescription or over-the-counter, should be in its original bottle and clearly labeled. Drug and narcotics laws are very strict in many countries, and you do not want to run afoul of them. Ask your dentist if it is advisable to have fluoride treatments, especially for children; most countries do not add fluoride to the water.

School records. If you have chosen a school for your child, you will probably have already made arrangements to forward your child's records. If not, be sure to request a complete set of records to take with you for each child. Don't forget school records, including diplomas and certificates, for yourself or your partner if either one of you might take continuing education classes while you're abroad!

Wills and guardianships. Your personal affairs should be in order before you leave. Your lawyer or a family member should have access to these documents in case of an emergency.

Power of attorney. Assign power of attorney to act in your interest at home, if necessary. (A power of attorney does not have to be permanent and can be nullified when you return, if desired.)

Paying bills. If you have a mortgage or other payments that must be paid while you're abroad, decide how to handle them before you go. There are several options, including maintaining a checking account at home and paying bills yourself, arranging for your bank to pay them (not all banks offer this service), or having your lawyer, accountant, or a family member pay them.

Travel advisories. The U.S. Department of State publishes a one- to two-page consular information sheet on each country that covers basic topics such as medical and safety information, as well as addresses and phone numbers of U.S. consulates in the country. When necessary, travel advisories are released regarding areas of political instability, terrorist activity, etc. Check before you travel. (Consular information sheets and travel advisories are also available on many on-line services, such as CompuServe, and at the State Department Web site at www.state.gov.)

Copy of important documents. Make two copies of important documents; take one with you and leave one with your lawyer or a family member. Important documents include:

- Passport (the inside front cover, which contains your passport number and other information)
- Visas, transit visas, and tourist cards
- Driver's license, international driving permit
- Insurance card and other information
- International Certificate of Vaccination, medical records

Special needs. If you or anyone in your family has any special needs, check that appropriate facilities and services are available from hotels and airlines. Not all are equipped to deal with infants, persons with physical disabilities, and other concerns such as medication that requires special handling or refrigeration.

Change of address. Be sure to inform all of the necessary people and companies of your change of address. Some companies will assess a service fee for mailing bills and statements internationally. Write to each company, and keep a copy of the notice in case a problem develops and to remind you what bills and statements you should be receiving. Don't forget the following:

- Banks where you are keeping local accounts or have loans
- Credit cards, including department store and gasoline cards
- Stockbroker or stock transfer agent, retirement account agents
- Lawyer
- Accountant
- Insurance company, including homeowners, personal, medical, and life
- Tax offices in any city or state where you have property-tax liabilities
- Voter registration office
- Magazines and periodicals
- Alumni association and professional memberships

Bank letter of reference. It is often difficult to establish banking services in a country where you have no credit history. It will help to have your bank or credit-card company write you a letter of good credit. Also helpful is a letter from your local office in your new country that states your salary. Some banks now have branches in many countries; you may be able to open an expatriate account at home before you go that will allow you access to bank services worldwide.

Close unnecessary accounts. However, you should leave open one or two key accounts that will provide you with a credit history when you return. Also make arrangements to terminate telephone, utility, garbage collection, newspaper delivery, and other services as necessary.

Inventory. An inventory of all of your belongings is helpful for shipping and insurance purposes. Enlist the help of an appraiser as necessary for items of value.

Packing. Put a card with your name and address inside each piece of luggage and each box being shipped. Don't put your passport in the boxes to be shipped!

BUSINESS AND
INFORMATION RESOURCES

U.S. Department of Commerce
International Trade Administration
Office of Latin America and the Caribbean
14th and Constitution, NW
Washingon, DC 20230
Tel: (202) 482–0305
Fax: (202) 482–0464

Mexico
Embassy of Mexico
911 Pennsylvania Avenue
Washington, DC 20006
Tel: (202) 728–1009
Web site: www.embassyofmexico.org

Mexican Consulates
There are many Mexican Consulates in the U.S. The
major ones are listed below; other locations can be found
by visiting the Web site of the Mexican Embassy at
www.embassyofmexico.org

Atlanta
2600 Apple Valley Road
Atlanta, GA 30319
Tel: (404) 266-2233
Fax: (404) 266-2309

Chicago
300 N. Michigan Avenue, 2nd Floor
Chicago, IL 60601
Tel: (312) 855-1380 or 855-0066
Fax: (312) 855-9257

Los Angeles
2401 West 6th Street
Los Angeles, CA 90057
Tel: (213) 351-6800 or 651-6825
Fax: (213) 351-6844 or 383-4927

New York
27 East 39th Street
New York, NY 10016
Tel: (212) 217-6400

United States–Mexico Chamber of Commerce
1300 Pennsylvania Avenue NW
Suite 270
Washington, DC 20004-3021
Web site: www.usmcoc.org/

American Chamber of Commerce of Mexico
A.C. Lucerna 78-4
06600 Mexico
D. F. Mexico
Tel: (525) 724-3800
Fax: (525) 703-3908

Belize

Embassy of Belize
2535 Massachusetts Avenue, NW
Washington, DC 20008
Tel: (202) 332–9636
Fax: (202) 332–6888

Costa Rica

Embassy of Costa Rica
2114 S Street, NW
Washington, DC 20008
Tel: (202) 234–2945/2946/2947
Web site: www.costarica.com/embassy/

Consulate of Costa Rica

There are many Costa Rican Consulates in the U.S. The major ones are listed below; other locations can be found by visiting the Web site of the Costa Rican Embassy at www.costarica.com/embassy/

New York
80 Wall Street, Suite 718
New York, NY 10005
Tel: (212) 509–3066

Los Angeles
1605 West Olympic Blvd., Suite 400
Los Angeles, CA 90015
Tel: (213) 380–7915
Fax: (213) 380–5639

Atlanta
1870 The Exchange, Suite 100
Atlanta, GA 30339
Tel: (770) 951–7025
Fax: (770) 951–7073

American Chamber of Commerce of Costa Rica
Tel: (506) 220–2200
Fax: (506) 220–2300
Web site: www.amcham.co.cr

El Salvador
Embassy of El Salvador
2308 California Street, NW
Washington, DC 20008
Tel: (202) 265–9671
Web site: www.elsalvador.org

American Chamber of Commerce
of El Salvador
Paseo General Escalón No. 5432
Tel.: (503) 264–7609
Fax: (503) 263–3237
Web site: www.amchamsal.com

Guatemala
Embassy of Guatemala
2220 R Street, NW
Washington, DC 20008
Tel: (202) 745–4952
Fax: (202) 745–1908
Web site: www.mdngt.org/agremilusa/embassy.html

American Chamber of Commerce of Guatemala
Tel: (502) 363–1774
Fax: (502) 367–3414
Web site: www.bcity.com/amcham2

Honduras
Embassy of Honduras
3007 Tilden Street, NW
Washington, DC 20008
Tel: (202) 966–7702

American Chamber of Commerce of Honduras
Tel: (504) 232–7043
Fax: (504) 232–2031
Web site: www.honduras.com

Nicarauga
Embassy of Nicaragua
1627 New Hampshire Avenue, NW
Washington, DC 20009
Tel: (202) 939–6570
Fax: (202) 939–6542
Web site: www.intur.gob.ni

American Chamber of Commerce of Nicaragua
Tel: (505) 267–3099
Fax: (505) 267–3098
Web site: www.amchamnic.com/index.htm

Panama
Embassy of the Republic of Panama
2862 McGill Terrace, NW
Washington, DC 20008
Tel: (202) 483–1407

American Chamber of Commerce of Panama
Tel: (507) 269–3881
Fax: (507) 223–3508
Web site: www.panamcham.com

Bureau of Consular Affairs
Tel: (202) 647–5225
Fax on demand: (202) 647–3000
Web site: travel.state.gov

U.S. Department of State
Office of Overseas Citizens Services
Tel: (202) 647–5225; (202) 647–4000 (off hours
and emergencies)
Web site: www.state.gov
Emergency information for Americans traveling
abroad, travel advisories, and background information.

U.S. Center for Disease Control
and Prevention
Tel: (404) 332–4559
Web site: www.cdc.gov
Health advisories, immunization requirements/
recommendations, advice on food and drinking water

Health Canada/Santé Canada
Laboratory Centre for Disease Control Travel Medicine
Program
Tel: (613) 957–8739
Fax on demand: (613) 941–3900
Web site: www.hc-sc.gc.ca
Health information for those traveling outside
of Canada.

Mexican Government Tourism Offices
Tel: (800) 44 MEXICO (446–3942) from the
U.S. and Canada.
Web site: www.quicklink.com/mexico/tourism/mgto's.htm

Panama
The American Society
Tel: 011–507 228–2331 or 011–507 261–2492

Inter-America Women's Club
Tel: 011–507 223–1749 or 011–507 269–7627

RESOURCES FOR MOVING ABROAD

Appliances Overseas
New York, NY
276 Fifth Avenue
Suite 407
New York, NY 10001-4509
Tel: (212) 545–8001
Fax: (212) 545–8005
Web site: www.appliancesoverseas.com
Household appliances and electronics that are
adapted or manufactured for international use.

Video Overseas, Inc.
601 West 26th Street
3rd Floor
New York, NY 10001
Tel: (212) 645–0797
Fax: (212) 242–8144
Web site: www.videooverseas.com
Household appliances and electronics that are
adapted or manufactured for international use.

Air Animal, Inc. (U.S. and Canada)
Tel: (800) 635–3448
Web site: www.airanimal.com
*Information and assistance on moving
your pet abroad.*

HELPFUL WEB SITES

Expat Access
www.expataccess.com

Escape Artist
www.escapeartist.com

Expat Exchange
www.expatexchange.com

SCHOOLS

International Schools Services
www.iss.edu
*The International Schools Services maintains a
listing of American and international schools in most
countries, and provides information and consulting
on international education.*

CROSS-CULTURAL RESOURCES

Terra Cognita™
www.terracognita.com
*Videos, books, audio, and Internet training and
resources for living and working in Central America
and around the world.*

Although a sizing conversion chart can be a step in the right direction, an accurate fit is found only by trying the item on, just as you would at home.

WOMEN'S DRESSES AND SKIRTS

U.S.	3	5	7	9	11	12	13	14	15	16	18
Continental	36	38	38	40	40	42	42	44	44	46	46
British	8	10	11	12	13	14	15	16	17	18	20

WOMEN'S BLOUSES AND SWEATERS

U.S.	4	6	8	10	12	14	16	18	20	22	24
Continental	32	34	36	38	40	42	44	46	48	50	52
British	26	28	30	32	34	36	38	40	42	44	46

WOMEN'S SHOES

U.S.	5	6	7	8	9	10
Continental	36	37	38	39	40	41
British	3½	4½	5½	6½	7½	8½

MEN'S SUITS

U.S.	34	36	38	40	42	44	46	48
Continental	44	46	48	50	52	54	56	58
British	34	36	38	40	42	44	46	48

MEN'S SHIRTS

U.S.	14½	15	15½	16	16½	17	17½	18
Continental	37	38	39	41	42	43	44	45
British	14½	15	15½	16	16½	17	17½	18

MEN'S SHOES

U.S.	7	8	9	10	11	12	13
Continental	39½	41	42	43	44½	46	47
British	6	7	8	9	10	11	12

CHILDREN'S CLOTHING

U.S.	3	4	5	6	6x
Continental	98	104	110	116	122
British	18	20	22	24	26

CHILDREN'S SHOES

U.S.	8	9	10	11	12	13	1	2	3
Continental	24	25	27	28	29	30	32	33	34
British	7	8	9	10	11	12	13	1	2

DISTANCE

1 yard	0.914 meters
1 foot	0.305 meters
1 inch	2.54 centimeters
1 mile	1.609 kilometers

1 meter	1.094 yards
1 meter	3.279 feet
1 centimeter	0.394 inches
1 kilometer	0.622 miles

SPEED

1 mph	1.609 kph
30 mph	48 kph
55 mph	88 kph
65 mph	105 kph
80 mph	128 kph
100 mph	160 kph
1 kph	0.622 mph
55 kph	34 mph
65 kph	40 mph
80 kph	50 mph
100 kph	62 mph
150 kph	93 mph

DRY MEASURES

1 pint	.551 liter
1 quart	1.101 liters
1 liter	0.908 dry quarts

LIQUID MEASURES

1 fluid ounce	29.57 milliliters
1 pint	0.47 liter
1 quart	0.946 liters
1 gallon	3.785 liters
1 liter	1.057 liquid quarts

WEIGHT

1 ounce	28.35 grams
1 pound	0.45 kilograms
1 gram	0.035 ounce
1 kilogram	2.20 pounds

TEMPERATURE

To convert Fahrenheit into Celsius, subtract 32, multiply by 5 and divide by 9.

To convert Celsius into Fahrenheit, multiply by 9, divide by 5, and add 32.

FAHRENHEIT → CELSIUS		CELSIUS → FAHRENHEIT	
-20	-28	-50	-58
-15	-26	-45	-49
-10	-23	-40	-40
-5	-20	-35	-31
0	-17	-30	-22
5	-15	-25	-13
10	-12	-20	-4
15	-9	-15	5
20	-6	-10	14
25	-3	-5	23
30	-1	0	32
35	1	5	41
40	4	10	50
45	7	15	59
50	10	20	68
55	12	25	77
60	15	30	86
65	18	35	95

FAHRENHEIT → CELSIUS		CELSIUS → FAHRENHEIT	
70	21	40	104
75	23	45	113
80	26	50	122
85	29	55	131
90	32	60	140
95	35	65	149
100	37	70	158
105	40	75	167
110	43	80	176
115	46	85	185
120	48	90	194
125	51	95	203
150	65	100	212
175	79	105	221
200	93	110	230
225	107	115	239
250	121	120	248
275	135	125	257
300	148	150	302
325	162	175	347
350	176	200	392
375	190	225	437
400	204	250	482
425	218	275	527
450	232	300	572
475	246		
500	260		

NOTES

NOTES

NOTES

NOTES